Lost

Inspiring Stories ....nties, Vol. II

Kyla Duffy and Lowrey Mumford

Published by Happy Tails Books™, LLC

Happy Tails Books™ uses the power of storytelling to effect positive change in the lives of animals in need. The joy, hope, and (occasional) chaos these stories describe will make you laugh and cry as you em*bark* on a journey with these authors, who are guardians and/or fosters of animals with disabilities. "Reading for Rescue" with Happy Tails Books not only brings further awareness to animal advocacy efforts, but each sale also results in a financial contribution to rescue efforts.

Lost Souls: Found!™ Inspiring Stories About Pets with Disabilities, Vol. II by Kyla Duffy and Lowrey Mumford

Published by Happy Tails Books™, LLC www.happytailsbooks.com

The publisher gratefully acknowledges the numerous rescue groups and their members, who generously granted permission to use their stories and photos.

Any brand names mentioned in this book are registered trademarks and the property of their owners. The author and publishing company make no claims to them.

Publishers Cataloging In Publication Data Available Upon Request

ISBN: 978-14904381-4-6

Visit the following link for more information about the dogs, authors, and rescues featured in this book:

http://www.happytailsbooks.com/about/authors/

Acknowledgements

Happy Tails Books would like to thank Cheryl Gustafson of "A Newly Created Page for Special Needs Animals" (Facebook) and our incredibly talented and giving proofreader, Charlotte Grider. Without these dedicated animal-lovers, this book would not have happened.

We'd also like to acknowledge the following pets and their friends, guardians, and photographers for providing us with photos for this book:

Front cover: *Dutchess*, Lisa Prince Fishler, printzphotography.com

Back cover (top): *Almendra,* Eli Hernández

Back cover bottom (from left to right): *Ty, Cali & Taffy, Kiefer, Zepplin*

Interior title page: *Bandit*

Introduction page (clockwise from top left): *Tito, Hailey, Nemo, Roxie, Scoot*

Table of Contents

Introduction: Building Community

With some dogs it's a toss-up as to who is master of whom, and who is best friend to whom. At least, that was the case with our blue Doberman, Buddha, an incredibly self-possessed being who took the attitude that eventually, she would get us fully trained. For years she had been my husband Eddie's guard dog, but then she softened and began serving as a nanny dog to our young daughter and the group of toddlers who came to our home for family daycare.

When Buddha lost the use of her rear legs at the age of 10 due to spondylosis (degenerative osteoarthritis of the spinal joints) and disc disease, we were faced with the choice of putting her through a risky surgery or euthanizing her. We could not afford the surgery, but to us, that wasn't a good reason to put a dog down. Since she was not depressed or in pain, euthanizing her was *not* an option.

We started Buddha on anti-inflammatories and decided to give her time to heal. In the meantime, we thought a wheelchair would be helpful in restoring her quality of life, though we struggled to find a decent design. As Eddie, a mechanical engineer by trade, began building her one, I became her servant, carrying her back end around in a sling and giving her massage therapy every night.

Eddie analyzed the canine skeleton and designed a cart that supported Buddha on her pelvic floor and had a yoke over her shoulders. This gave her spine the support it needed to heal. The cart was clunky by today's standards, but it allowed Buddha to walk in the woods and fields again. After several months, she rewarded us with her first steps on her own, without the support of the cart. There was a big lesson in Buddha's recovery about the value of convalescent care and perseverance.

Our vet was impressed with Buddha's recovery and began recommending us to people whose pets needed wheelchairs. With each cart Eddie crafted, he refined the original design to make it lighter and easier to use. When his own disabilities forced Eddie to leave corporate life, he decided to devote himself completely to helping disabled animals. A feature article in the local newspaper produced a spate of orders, and Eddie's Wheels officially became a business 10 years after Eddie built that first cart for Buddha.

That's when dogs *really* began ruling our lives. Our first local customers taught us that the spectrum of disabilities requiring mobility assistance was extraordinarily broad. KD, the Border Collie, wore her cart with a pool noodle strapped onto it so that she could go swimming. Voytek, the ancient Dachshund, needed a four-wheeler. Shala, the pup rescued from the town dump with missing front legs, inspired the first front-wheel cart. There were amputees needing counterweighted carts, arthritic dogs needing counterbalanced carts, and too many degenerative myelopathy-stricken dogs who needed carts that could be upgraded when their disabilities worsened. As the business grew, we hired more staff and developed carts with removable step-in saddles, variable axles, and detachable front training wheels for rehab. We even made some quad carts with head rests and tow handles in response to requests from people who needed these tools to manage their beloved pets' disabilities.

Over the years, we adopted several dogs who were in need of our carts. First there was Daisy, a delightful six-year-old Dachshund with four herniated discs, bladder and bowel incontinence, and a feisty, indomitable spirit that made dogs cower as she chased them in her cart. We learned so much from watching her slowly rehabilitate over time, gradually regaining function of her legs so that she could use her cart as a walker, propelling herself as she climbed hills. Daisy was an active, healthy dog on wheels for 10 years. She inspired thousands who met her at veterinary conventions, schools, and conferences to rethink their preconceptions about disabled pets. She died of a stroke on a snowy day in January at the ripe old age of 16.

Next, after a brief stint of fostering her for the New York City SPCA, we adopted Sweet Pea, a disabled, incontinent Pit Bull. As Sweet Pea's disabilities changed over time, we provided her with all kinds of canine rehab and physical therapy. An injury to her lumbar spine inspired an innovation in our carts that has since helped other animals: a tiltable, variable-angle saddle to compensate for "roached" posture. Sweet Pea was with us for six years, finally succumbing to cancer at the age of 12.

Willa and Webster came into our lives through Mutts N Stuff, a rescue group in Southern California that specializes in hard-to-place pets. Willa and Webster certainly fit the bill, as they were both born without forelimbs. We adopted them specifically because of this disability, as we were making many front-wheel carts and needed some personal experience with the challenges of using them. The pair has been a total delight as they have learned to be expert "drivers." How nice for them to be able to climb hills, sniff, play, and sit at will, instead of creeping along or hopping around like kangaroos!

Just a few months ago, a paralyzed Pit Bull puppy was brought in to be measured for wheels. We offered to adopt him and try to rehabilitate him; we felt that he was an assignment from Sweet Pea, whose cart fit him perfectly! We have since been working with the puppy, Beau, providing him with acupuncture, chiropractic care, physical therapy, and traction on our therapy stand, in the hopes that eventually he may walk again on his own.

Eddie and I truly live our life's work. Our motto, "We test our products on animals," speaks to our lengthy experience sharing our lives with disabled pets for the past 20-something years. Our business has grown, and we've added to our staff, but we still take each order individually with careful attention to ensure that every cart we build serves the individual's unique disability. We continue to be moved by the stories our customers tell us about their soul companions, and we feel privileged to be part of their lives.

 *Leslie DeGraff-Grinnell*

Inspiring Stories About
Pets with Disabilities, Vol. II

Gregarious Golden Girl

© Lisa Prince Fishler

D utchess' early life was not without challenges. At six weeks of age, she was bitten by a brown recluse spider on a digit of her left front paw. As a result, she had to have some tissue surgically removed, which left her with a permanently upward-pointing third digit. She was unique from an early age.

As Dutchess matured, her affection for people was reinforced by regular visits from neighbors. To call her hyper-social would be an understatement. Her affection for people (and their undivided attention) was—and continues to be—boundless.

Dutchess' formal training began when she was about six months old. She was quick to learn basic commands, and she developed a strong sense of confidence by interacting with other dogs and their handlers. Reinforcing her behaviors was easy, as Dutchess has always been extremely food-responsive. To this day, she will offer any behavior she knows in exchange for a fragment of cheese. (For a glob of peanut butter, she'll even invent new ones!)

During the next couple of years, Dutchess matured from a fiery puppy to a gregarious young dog. Over time it became increasingly apparent that, although she always got along well with other dogs, she preferred the company of humans. When Dutchess was six, a colleague told me about her dog recently becoming certified as a therapy dog. The program sounded just right for Dutchess, and shortly thereafter we enrolled her with instructor Susan Fireman.

Dutchess and I became a therapy dog team that May. Our first assignment was a challenging one. Susan felt that Dutchess' disposition would make her well-suited to work at the Anderson Center for Autism in Staatsburg, New York. She cited Dutchess' calm confidence and her ability to diffuse stress, and she was right; Dutchess instantly fell in love with her new job.

The following year, I began noticing some changes in Dutchess' vision. An opacity was forming in her corneas, and her irises were no longer responding to light properly. Her jovial attitude had not diminished, however. Dr. Cory Mosunic, a veterinary ophthalmologist, diagnosed Dutchess with pigmentary uveitis (PU), an inherited condition. Eye drops and oral medications slowed the progression of PU, but the disease would inevitably lead to painful glaucoma and blindness. Eventually, the appropriate treatment would be surgical removal of the eyes.

During the next five months, Dutchess and I made several visits to Dr. Mosunic's office, but her work at the Anderson Center continued without a hitch. She participated in fundraisers for rescue groups and was exceptionally pleased to attend my parents' 60th wedding anniversary party that October. As the sole canine among 75 human guests, she was in all her glory, receiving constant attention, affection, and food. She worked the room like a debutante, and no one noticed that she was nearly blind.

Though Dutchess was living in the moment at that time, I was thinking about the future and coming to terms with the fact that Dutchess would soon be completely blind. I began to teach her new commands to help her in her vision-reduced state (for example, commanding her to "step up" and "step down" when approaching curbs and stairs). I was able to maintain a balanced, calm attitude because Dutchess' attitude was joyful and positive, as it had always been, and because I knew that if I approached the situation as if it were tragic, Dutchess would absorb this stress, which would negatively impact her emotional and physical health. I realized that, while adjusting to her vision loss was challenging for both Dutchess and me, the bond between us would only be strengthened by the situation.

As the New Year approached, Dutchess began sleeping more and more due to the discomfort associated with her glaucoma. In January, I took Dutchess to visit Dr. Mosunic; together we decided that Dutchess' eyes needed to be surgically removed. Dr. Mosunic performed the surgery, and I could not have been more confident in her skills and in the decision that she helped me to make about the procedure.

Being without eyes clearly did nothing to dampen Dutchess' expressive personality. By all accounts, Dutchess was a model patient and a charming overnight guest at the hospital. Ten days after the surgery, Dutchess, with her perpetual squint (her eyelids have been permanently sutured closed), was back to fetching tennis balls in the snow-covered back yard, sniffing her way through her favorite activity. Two weeks later, she was thrilled to return to the therapy dog work that she loves so much. Participants at Anderson didn't judge or question her lack of eyes, and as always, they received the same unmitigated love in response. They interacted with her as they always had: as individuals who relish their time together with her when she visited each week.

Now 10 years old, Dutchess still leads a full life. We continue to volunteer as a therapy dog team, and she serves as an ambassador for HeARTs Speak, an organization of artists who use their talents to benefit shelter pets. Dutchess has her own book that shows how she, in spite of her vision loss, is able to help her human and animal friends recognize their strengths and use their talents to help others. She does K9 Nose Work and is a charter member of the Dog Scouts of America (DSA) Hudson Valley Howlers (Troop #223), an organization dedicated to fostering responsible dog ownership and celebrating the human-canine bond.

Together we attend numerous public events to advocate for animal-assisted therapy, autism awareness, and pet rescue.

People we meet are often moved by the story of how Dutchess has shrugged off the loss of her eyes and continued to be a giving, loving soul. Dutchess, through her perpetually joyful attitude, insists that no one pities her for her loss of vision but that they celebrate the good things life has to offer.

 *Mark Condon*

Untouched Spirit

© Gustavo Olvera

Although I have a career in a different field, I began taking classes at a veterinary school here in Mexico because I like helping animals. Sometimes I take care of animals dumped at the school by people who no longer want to care for them. On this particular day, a guy approached me and said, "Look! That lady has a puppy she wants to leave."

I told him that I already had enough animals, but I couldn't stop myself from looking anyway. When I saw her...what can I say? I fell in love with the little puppy, who had no arms and such a sad face. She was covered in open wounds from dragging her body around, and she could only move one of her back legs because the family "responsible" for her litter never helped her to learn to walk. The wound on her right elbow was so bad that I could see her cartilage. I put her on my lap, and she stained my pants with blood.

The hand-off from her former owner was strange. The woman gave her to me, and said, "Please take care of her." Then she started crying and ran away! I was left alone there holding this bloody puppy in my hands, thinking, "What is next?"

I have to confess that I spent a moment considering whether I should put her up for adoption or perhaps put her to sleep if she was suffering, but it didn't take long for me to realize that she was meant to be with me. She was so lovely, and her strength was inspiring. Her happiness and her will made me decide to fight for her.

I named the puppy Almendra because she was small, light brown, and sweet, like an almond, and I resolved to do whatever I could to help her to heal and to walk. Even though I had no idea *how* I was going to help her, I was not scared. I started looking for people with similar experiences and seeking out information on prosthetics. Here in Mexico, there are *no* options for canine front leg prosthetics, so I had to look abroad. I eventually found several devices, but they were big failures. From the first day, helping Almendra was a learning process.

While I continued my search for devices that could assist Almendra, I struggled to help her gain strength and mobility in her hind legs. In my city, there is not a single physiotherapist for dogs, so I had to look to YouTube and international clinics to learn how to give Almendra therapy. First, I started making bicycle movements with her legs. Then I massaged them and used a reiki (palm healing) technique. Finally, I bought a treadmill and held her chest while she practiced walking. We did that *every single day*. One day, after six months of treadmill therapy, Almendra started walking straight!

Helping Almendra's wounds to heal was a challenge. When she was a baby, I had to clean them and bandage them every day because when she peed and pooped and dragged herself around, she contaminated them. Keeping them from getting infected and trying to promote healing was one of my biggest challenges with her early on.

I continued searching for a device that could help Almendra walk more easily. Finally, we received an Orthopets Hoppy Vest, which straps around her chest to provide her with "front legs." When it arrived, I put her in it, and she started running! That was one of the happiest moments of my life, when all the therapy I did with her—all the days we spent using the running machine and all the cleaning and tending of her wounds—finally paid off. I just could not believe that after a year of hard work, we had succeeded.

Almendra is now a happy, healthy dog, just like any "normal" dog, and she is my greatest pride and joy. She is so lovely and so alive. Her smile is stunning, and her happiness is remarkable. Maybe she was abandoned; maybe she had no mobility; maybe she had open wounds and sores. But her spirit—that remains untouched. She is a fighter, and her will is so strong that she accomplishes everything she needs to. She is my hero, and she has changed my life completely. Now, when I graduate, I want to be a physiotherapist so that I can help more special-needs dogs to achieve their fullest potential and live happy, healthy, complete lives, just like my Almendra.

 *Adhara Talamantes*

Helping of Crepes

Before my husband and I were married, he lived alone, and I lived with my dog and three cats. Growing up, he'd always wanted a pet, but his parents didn't allow it. Just before we were engaged, we decided to foster a trio of kitties for Tree House Humane Society in Chicago so that he could learn how to care for them, and we could support the community we both loved.

Tree House called us one night and said they had three kitties who needed an emergency foster home. A kind lady named Rosa had been trying to trap them as part of the rescue's TNR (trap-neuter-return) program, but unfortunately, her neighbor had trapped them first and had taken them to a shelter that was about to euthanize them because they were feral and therefore "unadoptable." Rosa had hurried to the shelter and rescued them, but she couldn't keep them any longer, so that's where we stepped in. They arrived skinny and sick with eye infections and malnourishment. Additionally, one of them was missing a foot.

During the next six weeks, we spent much of our time caring for the kittens and providing them with as much love and attention as possible. The footless one was also the smallest, and she had the most health challenges. She wheezed constantly and couldn't breathe properly. She watched her brother and sister play and run around but couldn't keep up. I took to wrapping her up in my fuzzy robe and carrying her around the house. That made her feel warm and cozy, and it often put her to sleep.

After six weeks of watching the kittens play and grow, we decided that we couldn't let the little one go, so we officially adopted her and named her Crepes. Since then, she has grown up, learned to cope with missing a leg, and become a fully-functioning cat who needs very little help from us, other than the occasional comforting hug and spritz of anti-bacterial spray when she bumps her stump. Her breathing problems subsided with proper diet, and her eye infections went away, too.

Crepes has taught us that attitude is everything. I can't even imagine a world without her kind soul living, and it breaks my heart to think that it came so close to that. Now, Crepes is the spokes-cat for her own special-needs cat blog, where she disseminates information about special-needs animals and helps them find homes just like her own. She is a joy to both of us and reminds us every day that beautiful souls can arrive in any form, at any time, and we just have to be open to recognizing them.

 *Alana Grelyak*

No Pushover

One Indian summer day a petite, middle-aged Boxer found herself alone in California's big valley. This little fawn girl with white tips on her paws and a bit of white on her chest wasn't sure what to do, so she began exploring. Soon she became hungry and very thirsty.

Along the way, both of her hind legs became injured and very sore. So she curled up in a shady corner at a fueling station to rest and wait for the pain to stop. That's when someone saw her and took her to a Boxer rescue.

The rescue founder named her Lizzie and took her to a university veterinary hospital, where Lizzie was examined. Sadly, Lizzie's left leg was so badly injured that the experts could not save it. It was amputated just below her hip. Lizzie the "tripawd" went into a foster home to recover from surgery.

As Lizzie got comfortable in her new surroundings, her right leg got stronger. Things were going well for her until, suddenly, her foster family moved but didn't take her. With no other foster available, she moved into the rescue's kennel. Poor Lizzie's life was turned upside down again.

Wonderful people at the kennel took care of Lizzie. They walked her and gave her baths, treats, and cuddle time. Often, Lizzie rode in a car to rescue events, where she was a doggie ambassador. She met lots of folks and hoped to get adopted. But each time Lizzie went back to the kennel.

Hanging out with people was the highlight of Lizzie's day. While she waited for that special someone, Lizzie lost patience with the other dogs. A year passed, and she continued searching for a forever home. By then, Lizzie had three strikes against her: she was special-needs because of her missing leg; she was dog-selective because of her limited tolerance of other canines; and she was a senior.

The rescue founder took Lizzie home for the holidays. Lizzie let another dog boss her around that week because she was so happy to be in a home again. A photograph of Lizzie peeking through a wreath appeared on the rescue website, but after the holidays, Lizzie again returned to the kennel.

Living at the kennel was way better than being alone, but Lizzie longed for her own home. That spring she was the featured available dog on the rescue website, and she appeared in a television feature promoting adoptable animals. Lizzie's blast of stardom was exactly what she needed, and just before summer, she was adopted!

Unfortunately, her stay at her new home was short-lived because the family's toddler "had difficulty adjusting to her." Lizzie hadn't done anything wrong, but again, she found herself back at the kennel.

Meanwhile, a family that wanted a companion for their senior Boxer, Thor, contacted the rescue. They were specifically interested in saving a "less-adoptable" pooch and showed interest in several Boxers who were scarred, blind, deaf, shy, or older. Fortunately, they checked the rescue website right before their appointment to meet these dogs, and they saw that Lizzie was back and available for adoption!

When Thor and his family met Lizzie, she hopped around with grace and enthusiasm. She and Thor walked together and seemed to accept each other. When they stopped for a drink, Thor paced about before wandering back to Lizzie, who was lying down. Startled and perhaps intimidated by his approach, Lizzie barked firmly at Thor, which seemed to mystify him, but he let it pass.

They walked again before socializing a bit more. This time, the result was the same. Lizzie sat down, Thor sat next to her, and again she barked sharply at him. The rescue volunteers offered to introduce the family to a different dog, but after considering Lizzie's tragic history—alone and injured, losing her leg, bouncing between the foster home and the kennel, being returned—they didn't have the heart to leave Lizzie behind.

That is how Lizzie, the senior tripawd, found her forever home after 22 months in rescue.

Lizzie, who had lived most of her nearly eight years outside, was skeptical about living indoors with another dog. She had tried it once; why would this home or this dog be different? Would she go back to the kennel again? Lizzie was cautious. She was no pushover.

Lizzie decided to check the place out. She observed Thor. She explored the house at her own pace. She loathed the slippery floors that caused her to lose her balance, but the family quickly covered them in rugs as soon as they noticed her dilemma. She enjoyed walks and car rides, and soon she started following Thor everywhere; she became his shadow. Lizzie decided not to enter some rooms in the house, but the room by the front door became her favorite. She spent most of her time in that room and slept there every night.

Lizzie and Thor frequently went outside at night. Lizzie liked to breathe the night air, listen to the sounds, and sit in the cool grass. Thor patrolled the yard. Sometimes Lizzie and Thor got to ride in the car to the park, where Thor showed Lizzie all the awesome spots. They watched ducks in the pond and chased pigeons in the grass. Lizzie began to like Thor. He had the 411, and Lizzie did her best to mimic him (except when he jumped about tossing toys in the air; Lizzie didn't understand the concept of toys).

She appreciated the compassion this family shared freely, and one evening, when the lady of the house came home, Lizzie's heart skipped a beat! That was the moment when Lizzie realized that she loved this lady, and the lady loved her. Lizzie stood up and wiggled her little nub vigorously, and *her mommy* smiled before giving Lizzie a big hug and kisses. Finally, Lizzie *knew* she was home.

Despite this revelation, Lizzie was restless. She had fitful dreams that left her feeling thirsty and tired. She twitched, nodded her head in a strange way, and lost balance without warning. Her family was worried. The vet said Lizzie was experiencing seizures and provided her with medication to help control them, which she would have to take for the rest of her life.

At first, the medicine made her woozy. Poor Lizzie was sometimes unable to stand up after going potty. She always felt hungry, but she was getting too fat! The vet reduced her medication for a while and suggested that Lizzie eat some vegetables with her kibble. This helped her become stronger.

Lizzie ate her food, but continued to appear thirsty all the time. She had fewer seizures but acted grumpy. For example, she barked sharply at Thor one day when he surprised her while she was sitting with her daddy; boy, did Thor let her have it! He barked so loudly that she flinched, lost her balance, and fell. Lizzie barked again in fear, and Thor barked back. Then Daddy told them both, "Enough!" and they went to their doggie beds to pout.

Lizzie was very sorry and never got grumpy with Thor again. She shared her water bowl and her doggie bed with him. He looked out for Lizzie, and Lizzie loved him for it.

Then Thor got very sick and needed surgery. After that, he never accompanied Lizzie to the park again. Lizzie and Thor had their photo taken with Santa Claus, just before Thor went to the Rainbow Bridge.

Lizzie celebrated that Christmas and the next with her family. She enjoyed many adventures during that year: going to concerts in the park (she loved music); making friends with a horse, a rabbit, and two doggies in the country; camping; and even visiting the beach. Never did her family regret giving this special-needs, dog-selective senior a chance. The memories of the good times they spent together were well worth the small hurdles they had to help her overcome.

 *Bridget Conner*

The More the Merrier

Seven years ago, we had to watch our rescued Boston Terrier, Mr. Jiggs, cross the Rainbow Bridge due to congestive heart failure. Our Golden Retriever, Duchess, was somewhat lost without her buddy, so after several months of grieving, we decided it was time to get her a playmate.

We have always adopted rescues, so the obvious first step for me was to look at Petfinder.com to see who needed a forever home. I found a trio that the rescue group really wanted to keep together and realized how challenging that would be. It's hard to find a family to take three dogs at once, but on top of it, these dogs were two, four, and ten years old. Additionally, when I called about them, I was told that the 10-year-old, Benny, was almost completely blind from cataracts and most of his teeth had been pulled. He had severe nerve damage in his rear legs, so they didn't bend, and he had an awkward gait.

All three—Benny, Bette, and Barry (a.k.a Benny and The Jets)—had been spared from the pound by the Boston Terrier Rescue Club of Maryland. Who would be willing to keep the three together? We knew we could, and we *would*. There was no doubt—they would have a forever home with us for as long as they lived.

Dutchess and Bette fell in as friends right away, but Dutchess couldn't be trusted with the boys. It was a small inconvenience but not really a problem. Up went the baby gates and out went the pups in pairs to go potty. Over time, the baby gates came down, and everyone became best buds.

Benny needed to be carried down the steps to go outside, and he was very scared. Luckily, time helped him over his fear, and we felt that, for whatever time we had left to share Benny's life with him, it was worth the trouble of carrying him outside. We took Benny for many trips to an eye specialist to keep his eye problems under control, but one day he bumped into something and ruptured an eye. I called the specialist immediately and was told that his eye would need to be removed.

We knew that at 14, any surgery was risky, but we also knew that it was extremely rare for an eye in the condition of his to heal on its own. Nevertheless, we decided to wait and see what would happen, and we learned that our Benny was a real fighter! With lots of attention and eye drops, Benny not only kept his eye, but it healed, and we were lucky to have him—*all* of him—for another year.

Last year our little family started to fall apart as Duchess and Bette crossed the Rainbow Bridge. Old Benny was still walking around on his funny back legs that didn't bend, but finally, at 15½ years old, he indicated to us that it was time to help him cross the Rainbow Bridge.

Suddenly, Barry was all alone. Because it had been such a tough year, it would have been easy to say "no more dogs" for a while, but there are so many loving dogs needing homes. We found "twin" boys, Mikey and Poncho, through Boston Terrier Rescue of South Carolina. Now Barry and "The Twins" run, sleep, and play together.

In our experience, the old souls who need homes give their all to say "thank you." Nobody is too old or has too many issues. In fact, the bigger the problems, the greater the love that is returned; the rewards cannot be measured.

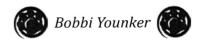 *Bobbi Younker*

Soul of a Poet

I never understood what I did to be worthy of his devotion, but I will cherish it to my dying day.

When I first met my handsome boy, I was cleaning his cage at the animal shelter where I worked. Two soulful brown eyes, in which I could see wisdom beyond youth, stared at me from behind a barricade of shredded newspaper. His start had been rough; he had been starved and beaten until neighbors stepped in and called to have him removed from his home. The animal welfare officer who brought him in refused to acknowledge the name his previous owners called him—Killer—so his cage card had a question mark where his name should have gone.

He was a German Shepherd-mix, but the rest of his heritage was elusive. Nevertheless, he was a handsome fellow with his pale blond face that highlighted his nearly ebony eyes, a black "saddle" on his back, and legs that he never quite grew into. I worked with him to make him adoptable, but when my co-workers tried to work with him, he had no interest in obeying the commands I had taught him. Clearly, he had chosen me, so there was no other option but to adopt this good-looking guy.

I renamed him Lancelot, and he turned out to be what everyone wants in a dog. He was intuitive, kind, and calm. When I would come home, his face would light up with a shining smile, and he would literally jump for joy. I never had to teach him to heel; I am convinced that I could have walked him off-lead during New Year's at Times Square, and he never would have left my side.

My mother, who had suffered two massive strokes in her mid-30s, said that she never believed in reincarnation until she met Lance. Even when she was having difficulty organizing her thoughts, Lance understood her, perhaps even more than she understood herself. There was no way that a human soul was not inside that doggie body.

At age 10, Lance started to limp. The vet kept insisting it was arthritis. As did another. And then another. After about a year, we finally found a vet with the real answer, an answer that dropped me to my knees. Lance had an incurable progressive paralysis that is heartbreaking and evil: degenerative myelopathy.

It was then that I was able to show Lance that his devotion to me was not unfounded. My husband and I became experts in the genetic disease. Lance received weekly chiropractic care and underwater treadmill therapy. We changed his diet. We added supplements to his food. We switched vets. We saw specialists. I firmly believe that our efforts pushed back the pace at which the disease developed.

With the heart of a warrior and the soul of a poet, Lance never let the slow paralysis of degenerative myelopathy affect his good nature or keep him from being "a dog about town." First a hip harness, then a cart, and finally, a red wagon helped him continue his adventuring. My husband I took Lance everywhere (everywhere that was paved, at least), and he showed us how to live with grace in the face of adversity. He never once freaked out when he couldn't move; he just waited patiently for me to move him, lift him, and carry him. But when his heartbreaking disease finally began to affect his lungs, we decided that it was time for him to run once more.

Our amazing vet and her staff understood our request to let Lance take his final breaths outdoors. On that day, the back of our SUV, which is usually crowded with cushions, two dogs and a red wagon, was suspiciously spacious due to the absence of the wagon that wouldn't be used again. Surrounded by love, Lance took his first unassisted steps in three years as he went across the Rainbow Bridge. It was the most beautiful but heartbreaking moment of my life when Tattoo, our yellow Lab and Lance's devoted companion, stood over Lance and cried his heart out—it was exactly how we all felt.

I am truly blessed to have been loved by such an amazing heart, and Lance will always be my "heart dog" for that reason.

 *Jeanne Poynton*

Special-Abled Anecdotes

What a Kisser! Milton the Chihuahua was found wandering the streets of Phoenix, Arizona, alone and starving at 10 years old. I saw Milton at the shelter and instantly knew many would overlook this special-needs senior. His bad back legs wouldn't hold him up very well, so he was scheduled to be put to sleep the following morning at 5 a.m. I took him home in the nick of time. I was happy to find that weebly-wobbly, four-pound Milton has a fearless attitude and childlike happiness. It took about a month for him to realize he was home, but now he gives me Chi kisses. Whatever time I have with him, I will cherish! -*Jackie Hartman*

Hiding Out

When you see a photo of my special Maltese girl, PrePre, you can't tell that she is differently-abled. We adopted her from a rescue group and quickly found out that her previous life had not been pleasant. She was so badly abused by her previous family (whom I don't think even deserve to be called her "family") that during her first days here, she hid from me—behind the furniture, in a corner—all for fear of being harmed. I decided to let her be, that she would come around on her terms. I knew she was eating, drinking, and using the wee-wee pads, but she would never do any of it in my presence.

Eventually, PrePre did venture forth, and 2½ years later, after much love, understanding, and patience, she comes to me to be petted and to be picked up to sit in my lap. She has come a long way, and I am amazed when I look at her and think of the scared, fearful, cowering girl she used to be. Every so often, PrePre still crouches in fear, but her anxiety is nowhere near as intense as when she first came to me.

PrePre is now a loving, sweet, trusting little one, who knows she is loved, safe, and provided for, with a warm bed, plenty of food, water to quench her thirst, and toys for her enjoyment. She brings a smile to my face each and every day, and quite often, as many who adopt query, I wonder who rescued who.

 *Patricia Miller*

Zip-a-Dee-Boo-Bah

My kitty, Boo, is just like any other kitty in many ways. I've had my black-and-white tuxedo baby since he was born. His mom was a stray who showed up at my dad's house one summer night, meowing on the porch. I had two other kitties and couldn't recognize the meowing, so I looked out the back door and saw Momma Kitty. When we saw that she was skin and bones with a protruding tummy, it didn't take much convincing for my dad to let her in.

Boo, along with his five siblings, was born inside a Christmas tree box in the middle of June. Of the kittens, Boo was the first to know his name, and he would run up to me when called. He was so cuddly and friendly that even my oldest cat, Buffy, tolerated him, and she hates everyone! It must have been his easygoing *purr*sonality that won her over.

The first two years were uneventful for Boo. His siblings found good homes. Momma Kitty and his one sister, Shadow, stayed with my dad, while his sister, Kalliope, came to live with us when we got a new apartment. So it was the four of us: Boo and his littermate, Kalliope; Luna, who was a year older; and Buffy, the grumpy one of the bunch who was six years older. We were a happy little family.

One day in May, things all changed, when I had the scare of my life. I came home and found that my Boo was having difficulty breathing. He was very lethargic. He had been coughing up hairballs lately, so I had been giving him hairball treatment. But this was clearly more than hairballs.

I called Banfield Pet Hospital, the only vet I knew would be open at the time, and they told me to bring Boo in, even though they were closing in 20 minutes. They were a half-hour closer than the closest 24-hour pet hospital, so I raced there in a panic. When we arrived, they put my baby on oxygen and worked to stabilize him, running tests to try and figure out what was wrong. At first, they prepared me for the worst by suggesting pneumonia or possibly another respiratory condition that could necessitate putting my not-even-two-year-old baby boy to sleep.

In the end, the results came back a little differently: Boo had asthma and a heart murmur. His asthma attack had been particularly bad, and putting him on oxygen had saved his life. Because of his heart murmur (on a scale of one to six, his is a four), he could not take the normal treatment of prednisone pills because it could cause heart failure. Boo's doctor recommended getting an Aerokat inhaler, which bypassed getting the steroid into the bloodstream and put it right into the lungs. Then, once they got him stabilized, they sent him to the 24-hour animal hospital to finish his treatment.

We spent six hours at the 24-hour hospital, and I could tell that Boo was tired from his ordeal. We were in the examination room for a long time, since there was an emergency case there that had to be dealt with, too. Boo lay on the table, and I put my head on the table next to him, holding his paw. Finally, the veterinarian came in and went over treatment options and specialists we could see. The vet administered the first of several doses of the Aerokat inhaler, gave me a prescription of prednisone just in case, and sent me home. Fortunately, I was able to take Boo home with me.

Caring for a cat with asthma and a heart condition, especially in a multiple-cat household, has been an adjustment, to say the least. In many ways, Boo behaves like a regular three-year-old cat. For example, he loves to snuggle, eat his kitty food and treats, and play with his favorite toys. However, we have to be very careful that he doesn't get too excited because over-stimulation can cause an asthma attack. If the attack is mild, I can treat it with the Aerokat inhaler, but because the inhaler acts as a trigger for anxiety, it often makes things 10 times worse. If the asthma attack is a bad one, I unfortunately have to resort to giving Boo a prednisone pill, even though it could adversely affect his heart. In those instances, it comes down to a judgment call: which is better for Boo's health: the anxiety and possible asthma attack from the Aerokat use, or the heart complications from the prednisone pill?

While people often think of "disabled" or "differently-abled" as having some sort of visible handicap, Boo is an example of the life-changing power of non-visible handicaps. I am constantly monitoring Boo to catch his attacks before they happen in order to keep his stress levels at a minimum. I only give him toys that don't make him too hyper (alas, that means no lasers). And Boo can't have any catnip. He gets all the toy mice he can handle, and he can play with zip ties to his heart's content, which he has adored since he was a kitten. For his birthday this year, he is getting a big bag of zip ties along with some freshly grown cat grass and some homemade cat food.

Despite his limitations, Boo is very content. He is still just as snuggly as ever with me and just as friendly with his sisters as he has always been. We just have to be a bit more careful now. And I am grateful that he is here. I honestly don't know what I'd do without my baby boy.

 *Shellie Smith*

O urs is a handi-capable home. We share our house with our human guardian, our mommy, and we refer to ourselves as "The Chew Crew." There are seven of us, and we are all special.

I'm Scoot. I was abandoned because I have a birth defect in my hind legs. I started using a wheel-cart for mobility when I was just three months old.

Next, there is Haley. She has a birth defect in her hind legs, too, but she can walk—sideways.

Mississippi was a puppy-mill breeding dog who came here emaciated after giving everything she had to her puppies. She's now my big sister.

Simmons has a deformed face and jaw, and because of that, no one wanted to adopt him. They thought that he was ugly. We don't see him that way, and all 135 pounds of him sleeps beneath Mommy's bed every evening. Did I mention that he snores?

Pan Pan came from a puppy mill. She is blind (though she still has one of her eyes), but she sees with her heart!

Miracle has no hind legs and was abandoned in a house. She now has her own wheel-cart and does pet therapy with me at our local hospital.

Last but not least is Athena. She was in the middle of the road when Mommy was coming home from work. No one stopped. No one cared. Now, Athena's job is to welcome new fosters and new family members into the Crew.

Yep, we are all pretty darn special. We all had nowhere to go. We were all unwanted. No matter. Now we are a crew—a family—and to me, that's a beautiful thing.

 *Scoot*

Adverse Reaction

The animal shelter named him Dusty. At nine months old, he was a beautiful mosaic of browns and tans with what looked like a black tire streak down his back. He was found tied to the shelter fence with chains around his legs, chains so tight that they cut into the side of his hind foot.

Our eldest son worked at a family restaurant with a woman who volunteered at that particular animal shelter. He had asked if she had seen any German Shepherds come in, and she told him about Dusty, a Shepherd/Chow-mix.

She said that the wound on his foot was not healing fast enough, so he may not be adoptable, but she would let us know in a few days. She gave him an application to fill out, just in case.

Soon the woman called to tell us that Dusty's wound had healed, and she offered to bring him by to meet us. He came for a home visit, and we could see that he instantly fell in love with our large property. At the same time, we fell in love with him, so two days later, Dusty came home to stay.

Dusty's name just didn't fit him; he was more of a Kozzmo. This handsome boy quickly showed us that he was loving and grateful, and he was *smart*. He learned any trick we wanted to teach him within two days and was very well-behaved. He even learned how to spell several words. Our 80-pound pup loved to go out in the yard and hunt; after all, the wild animals needed to know that this was *his* home now, not theirs.

Kozzmo was a happy-go-lucky guy, except when it came to veterinarians. Being treated for the cut on his foot left him with a significant distaste for them, and we had to try out five different vets before we found one he would trust. Kozzmo bit every single one of them and wouldn't allow them to treat him, until he met Dr. O'Connor, and the two of them came to an instant understanding.

When Kozzmo turned eight, he began having accidents in the house. We also noticed that he had an unquenchable thirst. We knew it must be diabetes. The vet gave us syringes and insulin, but three days later, Kozzmo lost all sight in his right eye and seemed to have very little in his left. We helped him maneuver around what he couldn't see, but he did pretty well on his own. Within a few months, he had his surroundings down pat, and you'd never know he was blind. Kozzmo continued to take his shots every day like a trooper and never complained.

Two years later, Kozzmo became arthritic in his back legs. He still didn't demand any help and did his very best to fight what was happening to his legs. He took medicine for the arthritis every day. When we had to help lift his hind quarters up the stairs because his legs really started failing, he accepted our assistance with grace and dignity.

Around the age of 12, Kozzmo started to get hard of hearing, and we noticed some dementia, but he was a fighter, and he still kept going. We built him a ramp so that he wouldn't have to go up and down the steps, and he carried on as best as he could.

Dr. O'Connor was amazed that Kozzmo was still going strong, and he teased Kozzmo about being a "wonder dog" who might become his oldest living patient with diabetes (in addition to all of his other ailments).

At the end of Kozzmo's 13th year, he developed a cough, which turned out to be fluid building in his lungs because his heart wasn't working well. This required that he take more pills. Then, on December 24th of that year, we went to pick up his insulin from the vet and arrived to see a black flag hanging on the door; Dr. O'Connor had died unexpectedly of a heart attack the week before. We were heartbroken. He was the most wonderful man and veterinarian. We didn't know where we would find another vet like him, a vet that Kozzmo would trust.

Kozzmo needed his medications, so we had to find another veterinarian—fast. We asked friends for referrals but ultimately went with one in the phone book that advertised that they "treat your pets like family." Since we do the same, we picked them. We called and explained our dilemma. The vet agreed to prescribe Kozzmo's medications over the phone, so we could get them immediately, but he also wanted to see Kozzmo as soon as possible. I requested a home visit, but the vet said that Kozzmo needed to be evaluated in the office because of all of his problems that needed attention. I knew it would be a disaster, but I made an appointment anyway for their latest time on Saturday so that both my husband and I could go with him.

We took Kozzmo to the appointment and were kept waiting for 40 minutes. During that time, Kozzmo became more and more anxious, upset, and uncomfortable. By the time the vet came in to see him, Kozzmo wanted out! His strong emotional response to being at the vet's office put him into cardiac arrest, and he didn't respond to the emergency treatment they gave him. He was getting worse by the second, and we knew that we had to let him go. No matter how much we would miss him, we didn't want to put him through any more anxiety, medication, or trauma. He would have only had a short time left anyway, maybe the two months until his 14th birthday.

Our hearts ached while we held him and comforted him as he went toward the Rainbow Bridge. We had to believe that Dr. O'Connor would be waiting there for him, a month to the day of his own passing.

From the time he came to live with us to the time he left us, Kozzmo's attitude did not change one bit. No matter what medical issues he faced, he always remained the same, happy, fun-loving dog. He was the best, and we miss him very much.

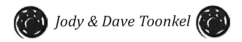 *Jody & Dave Toonkel*

Walk the Line

Having been abandoned as a puppy on a country road, our Labrador-mix, Cassie, was almost starved when we found her. Even so, she refused to be rescued until her brothers, who were there with her, were loaded into the truck first.

When Cassie was a year old, she was in an accident, and her back leg had to be amputated. Once we showed her that she could still do all the things that she had done before, she never let it slow her down. She had four more surgeries in her life for growths and tumors, even for one that was cancerous, but she always bounced back quickly!

Cassie loved children, especially babies, and she was always very careful around them. She loved cats and would adopt new kittens as her own. However, she was very protective of our cats and chased Orion, the neighbors' cat, away at every chance she got, even though I told her not to. One day, when our neighbor was moving, I told Cassie that Orion would be coming to live with us. She never chased him away again, and they became good friends!

Cassie was loving and nurturing toward other animals. For example, she once helped Huey, a neighbor's intellectually disabled dog, come home through the pasture. He could not walk in a straight line and would get lost on the way home. Cassie assessed the problem and simply walked with him, close to his right side, steering him in a straight path to his yard. She waited to make sure he made it all the way to his house before coming back home. Another time, she jumped into the pond and swam around and around behind a mother duck and her ducklings, nudging them with her nose if they stopped swimming!

I confess: Cassie also ran our household. She naturally took charge and kept us all on schedule. She was happy and healthy right up to the end. She died unexpectedly from an apparent stroke just short of her 13th birthday. Of course, we miss her terribly.

Bunny Dellinger

Rise and Shine

O ur kids finally convinced us to get a second dog, a dog of their own. Our other dog is great, but he clearly isn't our kids' dog. He tolerates them but doesn't actively engage them very often. They wanted a dog who would listen to them, play with them, follow them around, and snuggle with them in bed.

So we started looking for the perfect dog. We saw some great ones but never "our" dog. Then, one day we came across a listing of a beautiful Australian Shepherd-mix who had been rescued from death row at a county shelter. This 1½-year-old dog was described as being extremely affectionate. He loved kids and other dogs, and he was housetrained. I had a very good feeling about this guy, so an hour later we found ourselves at the dog's foster home. Twenty minutes after that, we had him loaded up into our car to take him to our house for a trial visit. We never took him back to the foster.

Welcome to the family, Wilbur! We found our perfect dog!

Well, almost perfect. He had a couple of issues that we knew about. One of his eyes was very cloudy, and his vision in that eye was minimal at best. He was also recovering from some sort of wound on his hip. Neither issue was a deal-breaker, but about 24 hours after Wilbur entered our lives, his energy level decreased, and he started limping and not wanting to put much weight on his back leg. After a little investigating, we discovered that he had been hit by car. It was time to get this dog to the vet to figure out what was going on.

At the vet, Wilbur's "few issues" blossomed into a bouquet of troubles. His cloudy eye didn't work properly and had glaucoma, an extremely painful condition that could only be cured by removal of the eye. There was also a good possibility that Wilbur had Valley fever, which is treated with years of medications that may or may not work. This infection, caused by the inhalation of fungal particles, zaps a dog's energy, which would certainly explain why a young dog like Wilbur was so mellow. Finally, the vet took X-rays and said that Wilbur had some soft tissue damage around his ankle, which should heal with time. At least there was that! Thank goodness.

The vet did find one more unexpected thing in the X-rays: shotgun buckshot pellets—a lot of them—embedded all over Wilbur's backside. When the vet showed me the X-ray, I counted more than 40 little pellets lodged inside of him. I had to take a picture of it, or nobody would believe me!

Before I got too freaked out, the vet assured me that it looked worse than it really was. He said that Wilbur had probably been shot long ago, so the pellets shouldn't cause him any other further damage. They weren't going anywhere. Apparently, the pellets were the least of his worries!

During that first visit, Wilbur achieved "rock star" status at the pet hospital. Everyone who worked there wanted to see the X-rays and meet the stray, blind-in-one-eye dog who had been shot and hit by a car but was still excited to give anyone near him a giant lick across the face.

Once home, I thought, "So, now what?" After five days with Wilbur, we were already smitten, but this was not how the adoption of our new friend was supposed to go. If we had known all of this beforehand, we probably never would have gone to visit Wilbur in the first place. Our kids were craving a vivacious, playful puppy, and we adopted a dog with a traumatic, mysterious past and an uncertain future. I wondered whether we should give Wilbur back and start over. I mean, that would be the "sane" thing to do, right?

I knew that returning Wilbur to his foster with his new, updated health records would render him practically unadoptable, but I wasn't going to force this dog on my kids. "It's the kids' decision to make," I thought, so I talked with them about the future removal of Wilbur's eye, the Valley fever (maybe he will kick it completely; maybe he won't), the ankle (which may or may not heal completely), and the 40+ shotgun pellets lodged inside of him. I explained the financial and emotional costs of keeping Wilbur and said that we would all need to make sacrifices.

The kids were very quiet while I explained all the facts. In fact, I'm not sure they have ever listened to me so carefully. (I only wish they would listen like that when I tell them to get dressed for school.) When I was done, they asked me several thoughtful questions, which I answered as honestly as I would have if an adult had asked me the same. I said that if it all sounded like too much, like it would be too difficult or too uncertain, we could give Wilbur back. I also said that alternatively, we could accept that Wilbur is already part of our family and only look forward to helping him have a better future.

It took them both less than three seconds to answer. Wilbur belonged to them. He wasn't going anywhere.

Now, you might ask, has this dog really been worth the trouble?

Like clockwork, every time I lay awake stressing out about Wilbur, I begin to hear the clanking of dog tags approaching. Moments later, Wilbur is on my bed snuggling with me. He tells me he's worth it. And in the morning, when it's time to wake up the boys for school, Wilbur jumps into their beds, licks them, and paws at them until they get up and rub his belly. This isn't something we taught Wilbur to do, he just insists upon it. He pushes open the boys' door every morning a few minutes before 7, as if he knows how to tell time. There's nothing better than the sound of giggling boys being happily awakened by their dog.

Wilbur's challenges aren't trouble. They are part of life. And Wilbur makes our lives better.

Wilbur has now been with us for several months. The eye has been removed; he's on Valley fever medication; his limp is gone; and he has more than enough energy (maybe a little too much!). He has transformed into the crazy, playful, loving puppy for whom we had been patiently waiting. I'm sure he is grateful that we chose to adopt him, but, truly, we are the lucky ones for having Wilbur in our lives.

 *Ari Lieberman*

All in a Tail

Nomi was born in a puppy mill cage and then transferred to a pet shop cage. He seemed healthy when he was purchased from the store, but at three months of age, he developed a progressive weakness in his legs, and before he could overcome it, he contracted parvo, a deadly virus that could have been easily prevented with proper vaccination. Needless to say, Nomi was a very sick puppy.

I happened upon Nomi at the rehab vet where we took one of our dogs. Now nine months old, he was on his third owner, who would leave him with Dr. Shaw during the day while he worked. Twice a week I would come into the office and see Nomi, lying helplessly behind the receptionist and just waiting to be picked up and petted. The nerve damage and the parvo had taken a toll, and he couldn't even lift his head. His front legs were locked at the elbows, and there was no muscle at all in his legs. To me, it was a bold statement about his personality that even though the rest of his body seemed not to function, his tail worked perfectly; this dog had an incredible zest for life despite his hardships.

I regularly picked Nomi up and played with him, and I quickly fell in love with him. One day Dr. Shaw told me that Nomi's owner was looking to give him up. Without hesitation, I said I would take him as long as my husband, Sean, agreed. Long story short, Sean came in to meet him and fell in love with Nomi just as quickly as I had. We met with the current owner and arranged to take Nomi home within the month.

That was five years ago. Nomi has gone through many treatments and therapies since then and has grown much stronger. Although he'll never walk, he can crawl across the room without a problem. We use a dog stroller to take him everywhere with us. When people hear Nomi's story, they often comment that they feel sad for him. We tell them not to; Nomi is alive, he is happy, and he is the king of the castle.

Julie Sosman

Fireball on Wheels

Although intervertebral disc disease (IVDD) is pretty typical among the Dachshund community, when it touched our lives, it turned our world upside down.

I was with our Dachshund, Sophie, when she "went down" (Dachshund speak for becoming paralyzed due to IVDD). She had an extremely severe case of disc herniation, which led to a stage-5 spinal cord injury with a loss of deep pain sensation. I provided her with the recommended emergency surgery, and, initially, she was given a 95% chance of a full recovery. Even so, she remained completely paralyzed. The letdown I felt when I received her prognosis is indescribable. I resented being part of that 5% minority and held on to a lot of anger about it for a long time.

At the time of Sophie's injury, my children were one and three, and they still seemed like babies. I was a busy and often frazzled stay-at-home mom, who most days could barely keep my head above water, let alone keep our house clean. Now, here I was, in the blink of an eye faced with helping my beloved and cherished Sophie through the most difficult and dreaded challenge of her life on top of my usual overwhelming duties. My husband and I had absolutely no experience in caring for a pet with special needs, nor did it seem like we were in the stage of our life to provide for her. Despite that, there was never a question: I knew from the first moment she became paralyzed that we would keep her no matter what. But we definitely had questions about how.

As it turned out, those questions were quickly answered by Sophie herself, as she guided us through her recovery and showed us the power of acceptance and positivity.

Being a Dachshund lover, I had heard stories about IVDD but was completely unaware of many aspects of the condition. For one, I had never connected the dots between a spinal cord injury and incontinence, so Sophie's incontinence was both unexpected and terrifying. One of the most difficult things was trying to provide others with answers regarding her incontinence when I wasn't even sure of the answers myself. The response I received from many people about this new facet of our lives was very negative, and perhaps that fueled me to become even more determined to find ways to adjust to Sophie's incontinence. In the end, Sophie and I proved all of the negative people wrong, as the incontinence aspect of her disability has proven not only to be easy to cope with but, at times, even convenient. That I can express her bladder when and where I please meshes with our lifestyle, and doing this simple thing for her to help her live in comfort has become my pleasure.

Before Sophie became paralyzed, I had never seen or heard of a dog wheelchair, but one evening, when Sophie was still in the veterinary hospital recovering, my sister called to tell me about a website that sold such things. The moment I opened the web page, I was overcome with an overwhelming feeling of hope and comfort, knowing that wheels were available for her if and when she needed them. At the time, I couldn't have known how wonderful and integral to our lives those wheels would become.

Just a few short weeks later, Sophie received her own wheels. She quickly became "our Dachshund, Sophie" again, doing all the things she enjoys most in life: going for walks, chasing the squirrels, and patrolling our backyard. Her new mobility was effortless. These wheels allowed her to continue leading the way on our walks and breaking into a run when she felt the need to move. She just rolled over curbs, sticks, roots, and whatever else got in her way. To this day, she's a little fireball on wheels, a typical Dachshund who makes her voice heard and holds her head up high; her confidence never wavering.

While at first we wondered whether we would be able to help Sophie surmount her new challenges, we have come to see our journey with her as one of the biggest blessings of our lives. Through Sophie's zest for life, her tenacity to heal and move on, her positive attitude, and her acceptance of the hurdles that life has put in her way, Sophie teaches my children important lessons that I would never be able to teach as effectively on my own.

I have personally been humbled by Sophie's sacrifices and inspired by her attitude so much so that I felt compelled to achieve my own lifelong dream. After working through much of my anger about Sophie's paralysis, I started blogging to share her story with others. I had never done anything like that, though I had fantasized about being a writer all my life. Sophie took me out of my comfort zone and gave me the motivation and reason to follow this dream. Since then, writing has become my passion and has served as a healthy coping mechanism as I search for the meaning behind this tragedy.

My life will forever be enriched by this experience of living with and caring for Sophie; my only hope is that I can give back all she has given to me.

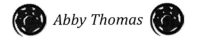 *Abby Thomas*

No Sea Creature

Nemo's story starts in November 26th of last year, when he was the "only child" born from a C-section. He was backward and upside down in the womb and had ectrodactyly, or "lobster claw," which affected his right front leg. Nemo's breeder, Brenda, did not believe in destroying puppies due to special needs, so she put Nemo up for adoption. Brenda corresponded with some people who were interested in Nemo, but they walked away as soon as they found out about his special leg.

We had recently lost our beloved dog, Feliz, to cancer and were looking for another dog to help our Jack Russell, Little Bit, get over her depression from the loss of her friend. I came across Nemo's picture online, and it was love at first sight!

When we contacted Brenda, I had no idea what kind of "special need" Nemo had, but when Brenda told us about Nemo's front right leg being shorter than his front left one and permanently bent at a 90-degree angle, I asked, "That's it?"

So what if Nemo had a short, bent front leg? He was just too adorable for something like that to keep us from adopting him.

We had a bit of a hurdle in getting him to us, since Nemo was in Wisconsin, and we live in Florida, but we made arrangements to meet Brenda in Louisville, Kentucky, since she was going there to show her dog and Nemo's Father, Dune, that week. It was a good central meeting point. We took our time getting there, so the trip took a total of four days for us, but that included stopping to see family along the way.

Nemo was three months old when we picked him up. Two months later, we have discovered that he is a holy terror and full of energy; he really has no idea that he's different. He runs and jumps just as fast as any dog I've seen, and he's even more agile than some.

I can't believe that someone else hadn't adopted him before we found him, but I'm glad it turned out this way. Our lives are so much better for it. Nemo has taught us a lot, and surely we have more to learn from him! We are planning to help Nemo become a therapy dog in the future, but for now, his being our loving family member, our boy, is enough.

 *Matthew Kines*

Out of the Barn

I found Teddy when he was an 11-week-old kitten with a horrendous upper respiratory infection. His litter was born as barn cats, so they were all outside. As a delivery driver, I saw kittens at a lot of stops, but this little guy left an impression. He was just sitting there staring at me, though he couldn't see much of me with the ulcers he had in both eyes. I'll never forget that, as he stared at me, his mom stared at him as though she was willing him to look pathetic so that I would take him home.

I couldn't get this little kitten out of my mind, so I went back and left the property owners a note. They called me that evening, and I asked about him. They said they couldn't afford to take him to the vet, but they were trying to keep his eyes clean. I called my vet, Dr. Tracy, and told her I was going to get a stray the next day. Could I bring him there first thing? Of course, she was happy to oblige.

The next day, I went back and picked him up. I had to work, so my mom met me and took him to the vet. According to my mom, he was very quiet on the ride there. Dr. Tracy said she didn't know if he would make it, but she would try to help him.

While working the next day, I got a call from Dr. Tracy, and she said she could tell as soon as he started feeling better because he began yowling. All during the call, I could hear the kitten hollering. Teddy tested negative for all the bad stuff (like feline leukemia), so he would be safe to introduce to my current critters (three dogs and two cats).

Teddy may have been out of the barn, but he wasn't out of the woods. He was still dehydrated, wormy, and slightly emaciated. His still had an upper-respiratory infection and ruptured ulcers in both eyes (two in the right and one on the left).

At least he was in good hands...or paws, rather. As soon as we got home, my dog Takoda decided he was her baby! She kept his face and ears clean whether he liked it or not, and to this day, they still sleep together. Though Teddy is blind in his right eye and has limited peripheral vision in the left, he has grown into a beautiful Abyssinian who looks just like his mom.

 *Kelly Rambo*

Under the Trash Heap

© Shanna Wilkinson

hree years ago, a good Samaritan pulled over to pick up a pile of trash on the side of the highway. Under the garbage was a skinny, matted, scared, little black dog who had been hit by a car.

The good Samaritan rushed the dog to the emergency vet where his front leg was amputated. Sheltie Rescue of Utah took him into their rescue program, and Cassidy found his forever home with me.

After I adopted Cassidy, he had a lot of medical problems that stemmed from the amputated leg. With many visits to the vet and additional surgeries, Cassidy is now happy and healthy, and he has set out to make a difference by being an advocate for special-needs rescues. Together, we share the message that every life has value.

Our presentations for children are mainly about accepting that everyone is different and special and that each one of us has something positive to give to the world. To this end, Cassidy demonstrates how his disability does not stop him from making people feel good. When he walks into a room, people sometimes don't know how to react, but his loving, trusting nature quickly puts everyone at ease. He snuggles into each person's arms and shows them that he is not a disposable piece of trash; he is perfect the way he is, and through his affection he assures them that they, too, are perfect the way they are.

Cassidy and I also visit rehabilitation centers, where we work hard to give people hope. Cassidy's story reinforces the message that love conquers all and that hope and perseverance are powerful forces in rehabilitation and recovery.

Who would have thought that such an amazing dog could be found under a pile of trash and go on to touch so many lives?

 *Kathy Cain*

Gallant Little Trooper

After I had major surgery, my doctor wanted me to start walking to improve my health, so I looked for a dog to go with me. I found a one-year-old Corgi/ Shiba Inu-mix at a local shelter on Wednesday and brought her home on Friday. I named her Meaghan.

Meaghan was so terrified of being abandoned again that she had to be coaxed outside to go potty. The sight of a leash sent her into hiding, and once attached to one, she refused to walk through any door. With some suggestions from a dog trainer, I finally got Meaghan to walk on leash, but at first, she wouldn't go potty on walks, even after all night in a crate. Eventually, she would stroll with great enthusiasm.

I kept working on Meaghan. Gradually, she blossomed and showed me that she was house-trained and crate-trained and had been to obedience training.

When Meaghan walks, her back end sort of "rumbas" along, so it always looks like her tail is wagging. And her perky ears and face make her seem like she is smiling. People frequently stop me and ask if they can pet her. She's happy to oblige, and even more so if someone is willing to throw a ball. All the other dogs used to chase her at the park as she tore after the ball, and she would tell them off if they got in the way while she was "working" at getting that ball back to me. Once she figured out that walks are fun, she started trying to herd me out the door every morning, talking to me if it seems I might be forgetting that her job is to take me on walks.

One day, Meaghan started limping, so off to the vet we went. She was diagnosed with two torn ACLs (knee ligaments), which would cost $2,000 to fix. That was beyond my budget, but Meaghan still wanted to walk. We walked as far as she could, maybe just past three houses. Then she would sit down to tell me she was done. Since she was too heavy to carry very far, I found a free baby stroller to which I added a kennel pad, so I could lift her into the stroller and roll her home. The little walks grew longer and made her strong again; a year later there was no evidence of her injury.

Meaghan is usually a great car travel companion. She sits or lies quietly in the passenger seat and never makes a fuss. She has visited Los Angeles, California, several times and Seattle, Washington, and Dallas, Texas, three times each. But one day in the car, Meaghan reminded me that her spirit was still as fragile as her ACLs. Everyone in the house was sick with colds, coughing all the time. I decided to drive the car instead of walking the whole way to her favorite place to dig holes. I put her in the car, and all of a sudden, she started shivering and shaking with fear. She tried to hide in the back and put her head under things. The atmosphere of illness or perhaps the noise of the coughs must have reminded her of her past. Maybe her previous owner had died from a respiratory illness just before she was abandoned and landed in the shelter. Since that car ride, Meaghan sometimes shows fearful behavior when first put in the car, but then she relaxes and enjoys the ride.

Meaghan is now 12 years old, and she is clearly grateful that she was rescued. Every week, she "pays it forward" by visiting seniors in a care hospital, where she snuggles with them on their beds. They look forward to her visits, and the staff, doctors, therapists, and paramedics also enjoy her smiley face and wagging tail.

Meaghan is my gallant little trooper. Wherever I go, she follows, but hidden away is the great fear that she could be abandoned again. As for her knees, I monitor her activities carefully. I don't let her do stairs, and I limit her digging. I have ramps so that she can get into the car by herself and up onto the bed. Our walks are not as long as they used to be, but that doesn't matter. We just enjoy each other's companionship, as we have for the past 11 years.

 *Jane Fisher Urbach*

Special-Abled Anecdotes

Two Peas in a Pod: When Snoopy was three weeks old, his mom was hit by a car and killed. Their family asked us if we would take him. They had come to the right place! Despite living on a tight budget, we never hesitate to take in a special-needs dog, and we always make it work. Additionally, while my husband works, I stay at home to care for my 26-year-old son, Evan, who has muscular dystrophy, learning disabilities, and hearing impairment. We quickly discovered that Snoopy was deaf and trained him with hand signals instead of verbal commands. We came to find out that Snoopy is the smartest dog we have ever had! He's Evan's best friend, and he guards his family and our four acres with his life. Nothing gets past him, and we're extremely glad that his family passed him along to us! - *Sherry Jolly*

Handsome Gentleman

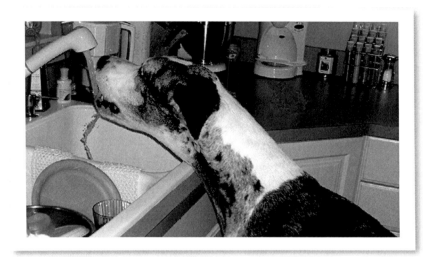

Jake came to Harlequin Haven Great Dane Rescue at seven years old, when his family was moving and did not want to take him with them. Not only was Jake considered a senior, but he was also in very bad shape physically, so the cards were stacked against him. We assume he must have spent quite a lot of time in a crate, as he had almost no muscle development in his rear legs. This caused him to walk with his back hanging quite low and his knees constantly bent. But despite losing the one family he had known since he was eight weeks old and having lived a life where he was obviously neglected, he was the sweetest dog I had ever known.

I will never forget the day I first met Jake. When I walked in to volunteer at the rescue's kennel, he greeted me instantly with a wagging tail and a shower of kisses, as if we were longtime friends. The sight of him was heartbreaking, but at the same time, his spirit was much more alive than most dogs who wind up homeless for reasons they cannot begin to understand.

I left the rescue that day with a heavy feeling in my heart, and I could not get Jake out of my head. I am often confused about how dogs end up at Harlequin Haven, as most are wonderful and possess the qualities that make a great canine companion. After spending just a few hours with Jake, I was more confused than ever because of his amazing personality and the love he wanted to share with everyone who came into his world.

As I continued my volunteer work at the rescue, I found myself falling more in love with Jake with each visit. I was recently divorced and was on a very tight budget with two other Great Danes and a yellow Labrador at home, so the last thing I needed was another dog. But I could not stop thinking about the unfair life Jake had already lived and the fact that he had very little chance of getting adopted due to his age and condition. I struggled with the thought that such a wonderful dog might live out the rest of his days confused in a kennel. So, despite most of my family and friends strongly discouraging me to do so, on hot day in late August, I brought Jake home with me so that I could show him what it was like to be truly loved.

After adopting Jake, I took him to my vet to find out how to help him get around better and to make sure he was not in pain. To my surprise, I was told that his condition was too far gone and that at his age, there was no chance for improvement. The vet said I should not expect him to live more than six months. Obviously, I was already attached to Jake, and there was no way I was going to give up on him that easily.

I made an appointment for Jake with an orthopedic specialist to get his opinion on how I could help Jake to walk better. Once again, I was shocked to hear the same prognosis, which was that Jake would never make it to his eighth birthday, so I should shift my focus to making him comfortable. My heart ached, as I could not imagine losing him so quickly after he finally had a chance at a great life. I could not accept this fate for such an incredible dog, so instead of despairing, I challenged myself to do all I could to improve his health and give him the best life for whatever time he had left on this Earth.

I knew I could not push Jake but thought that if he was willing to walk with me and even climb some steps, I could possibly help him build some muscle in his rear legs, which would help him to walk better. It turned out that Jake was more than willing to participate in anything I asked of him. We started taking daily walks, slowly increasing their length. Gradually, I began carefully guiding him up and down stairs. It was not long before I noticed his back rising up and his knees straightening out. Jake loved the time he and I spent alone together, and I could see him getting a little stronger with each day that passed. Before my eyes, he transformed into a tall, healthy, gorgeous Great Dane, standing proudly at 39½ inches from the ground to his shoulders.

His personality also blossomed with each day, as his body began to work with him rather than against him. From the first day, he was wonderful with my other dogs and with everyone he met. But the more time I shared with him, the more I found out that Jake's spirit and will to live were stronger than any human or dog I had ever known. No matter what came his way, he constantly had a positive attitude and wanted to do whatever it took to make me and everyone around him happy. I began to call him my handsome gentleman to reflect the incredible dog he was becoming.

The six months the veterinarian predicted turned into four years when Jake celebrated his 11th birthday with me. It was a day I thought we would never share. Unfortunately, a couple of months later, Jake's health started going downhill, and his mobility gradually diminished. Even though his body had begun to fail him, his spirit never faltered. He still wanted to do whatever he could to enjoy his life and bring a smile to my face.

After many sleepless nights, I finally decided it was time to send him to that most peaceful and happy place, the far side of the Rainbow Bridge, and make him whole again. It was beyond heartbreaking to make this decision, but I knew it was what I owed him after all he had given me in the past four years. On Oct 31st of his 11th year, I said goodbye knowing that he would once again be able to run and play with all the other animals at the Rainbow Bridge.

Jake came along at a very difficult time in my life and turned out to be exactly what I needed. Up until the very end, he continued to be a positive light that gave me hope every day. I still miss him more that I can express, but I will forever be grateful for the time I shared with him and all he taught me about life, love, and happiness.

 *Christe McGarry*

No Small Inspiration

My precious Mia, a Chihuahua, was born with a cleft palate—the two plates of the skull that form the roof of her mouth were not completely joined. Mia had several surgeries, but they all failed to correct her deformity, and even the top universities gave her little hope of survival. This congenital disorder often takes lives by allowing food contents to enter the lungs, which ultimately causes aspiration pneumonia.

I refused to give up on Mia and vowed to fight for her for as long as *she* continued to fight. In the end, it was pneumonia that took her life two months short of her second birthday, but she lived every day before that to the fullest. She faced many medical obstacles but never let them overpower her love for life.

We decided to do our best to make something positive out of Mia's tragedy, so we created a foundation to share her story and to inspire people to adopt animals with cleft palate and other birth defects. Through the Mia Foundation, Mia has given hope and inspiration to people around the world. Our mission statement is this: "If they are born, they deserve a chance to live!"

On this journey, I have come to believe that Mia was sent here to help us all by demonstrating courage and unconditional love and by teaching us to never give up, no matter what obstacles we may face. She has inspired many to be brave, to be strong, and to smile in the face of adversity. Most importantly, she taught us love!

 *Sue Rogers*

Misfit Manor

I witnessed a Thanksgiving miracle: my dog, Baxter, took tentative, wobbly, awkward steps with his paralyzed back legs.

The Tuesday before, I had glimpsed some movement. On Wednesday, my partner, Brian, saw the same thing. On Thanksgiving morning, Baxter managed to right himself and began taking some steps.

This is definitely something for which we are thankful.

We had adopted Baxter, a three-year-old Shih Tzu, from the local SPCA. His background is a mystery. Since he had little musculature in his back end, doctors assumed that his spine had been injured some time ago and that the damage was irreversible. He was originally scheduled to be euthanized, but after a caring veterinarian built him a makeshift wheelchair, he was given a new lease on life.

After Baxter was offered for adoption, many people expressed interest in Baxter but left abruptly when told he was paralyzed. Brian and I started receiving messages from concerned friends soon after this. They told us we were the only ones who could save this dog. We already have a house full of misfit animals, so what was one more?

We went to see Baxter at the shelter. He was terrified, shaking pathetically in the back of the cage. We could not leave him there, so after paying a small adoption fee, we walked out with him. No questions asked, no background check. They were glad to get rid of him.

The first week was difficult for Baxter. He was sullen, but as soon as he got in that cart, his tail (which, by the way, works just fine) wagged and wagged. He became confident and social. He started looking us in the eye. After a few weeks, he decided a house of full of crazy animals and a few people was not so bad after all.

We took Baxter to a specialist and learned about exercises that would strengthen his legs. Then we took him home and started working with him, which brings us to Thanksgiving—when he took a few steps, and we witnessed our miracle!

 *Domenick Scudera*

Trailer Treasure

A young Boston Terrier was found in a dumpster at a trailer park near Lebanon, Tennessee, a little more than a decade ago. Since he had been born with a neurological birth defect that caused paralysis in his back legs, some very sick person decided to throw him away like a piece of trash.

An 18-year-old girl from the trailer park rescued him and immediately called Boston Terrier Rescue of East Tennessee (BTRET), which at that time, was a new rescue organization (BTRET has since saved the lives of almost 1,500 other southern Bostons). The next morning, the president of the rescue, Joe, picked the dog up, took him in, and named him Harryman, and for the next year, he provided Harryman with some very special care.

We found Harryman on the BTRET website one Monday in May of that following year, and later that week we drove five hours south from Owensboro, Kentucky, to Maryville, Tennessee, to meet the legend known as Harryman. Needless to say, his courage and spirit immediately stole our hearts! We adopted him that afternoon and took him to his new home.

Caring for Harryman is much like caring for a special-needs child. We carry him in and out of the house several times each day. Because of his small, frail torso and crippled back legs, we have to physically support him during all of his outside activities. As for walks, he goes with us in a special stroller that was given to us by a caring neighbor.

Harryman has taught us more about courage and unconditional love than any human in our lives. In addition to his birth defect, about three years ago he developed ulcers behind both eyes. Two veterinary specialists told us we would either have to extricate his eyes or put him down. We prayed several times about Harryman's quality of life after this type of surgery, and God's answer came quickly. We removed his eyes and continued loving him as we always had.

Harryman is now nearly 12 years old, blind and crippled, but in very good spirits and health. He still army-crawls from room to room, and he now uses his senses of smell and touch to guide him to his food, water, toys, and bed.

One other major setback came for the little guy when in August of last year, he lost his cuddle buddy and best friend,

Kidd Rock (also a special-needs Boston Terrier), whom we adopted from the Southern Cross Boston Terrier Rescue in Nashville, Tennessee, and loved for nine years until a brain tumor took him from us. Harryman was not the same for quite a while, but his spirit and energy have finally returned. Now, he plays every day with his new rescued friends, Molly and Ziggy.

Harryman is truly a remarkable Boston Terrier. He has taught us so many life lessons that we are in the process of writing a children's book about him, so he can continue to inspire others, even long after he's gone. We hope the book will raise awareness about special-needs dogs and raise money for rescues. It's the least we can do—Harryman has given us so much, and we want to give something back.

Harryman is truly our *hero*!

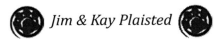 *Jim & Kay Plaisted*

The Gift that Keeps Giving

For some reason, Christmas makes me feel depressed, perhaps because many people seem more involved with the busyness of the season than with the true meaning of the day.

But last Christmas was different. And it was wonderful.

I got home from work early on December 21st and began to check Facebook postings. One of the first posts I noticed was a picture of a dog lying in the snow. He looked miserable.

The note from a woman named Cynthia said he was a stray with no collar or tag, and nobody seemed interested in claiming him. I was immediately drawn to this dog. I told my wife I just had to try to save him.

The next message about the dog noted that he was very old and did not move very well. His nose was running and he had a cough. There was considerable hair loss on his back. His ears had thick pus running out of them, and the fur around them was matted. From the picture, I could tell he had cataracts.

A short while later, Cynthia posted a video of him, and I noticed he had a disturbing cough. He seemed to be trying to loosen phlegm without success. Seeing him in this condition broke my heart. Luckily, my wife understood my feelings and quickly agreed to my applying to adopt him.

Cynthia knew the ins-and-outs of dog rescue, so in order to ensure that this dog went to an appropriate family, she worked with a local rescue to have us evaluated upon receiving our application. The rescue already knew me as a transport volunteer, so we were approved quickly, and they helped me make arrangements to pick him up the next day. In the meantime, Cynthia took him to a local vet to get him started on treatment.

I made the four-hour trip, and the first thing I thought when I met him was that he looked terribly sick. Somewhere in there was a beautiful Norwegian Elkhound, but he was so thin that his ribs were showing. His fur was matted, and he was extremely dirty. On the ride home, I would find out that he also smelled rather nasty from the ear infection and rotten teeth.

Despite the dog's appearance, I was already in love with him and wanted to get him home to start making him feel better. On the way, I stopped at a McDonalds and shared a cheeseburger with my new pal. The emaciated dog was terribly hungry, so that perked him up a bit; I think it was our bonding moment.

Once home, I put him right into a bath with medicated shampoo for his chewing lice (the cause of his hair loss). Of course, I did not want our other six dogs to be exposed. This dog was so weak that it was hard to get him to stand up long enough to clean him, and I had to carry him everywhere. He slept a lot.

On Monday, December 24th, we took our new dog to the vet, where we decided that once the infection was cleared up, he would be neutered and have his teeth cleaned and/or extracted. The vet guessed that he was between 14 and 16 years old and thought he was almost completely deaf.

My wife decided to call our new dog Winston after Winston Churchill because he was old and distinguished. He responded to the medication and looked better each day. He gained the weight he needed, his eyes became brighter, he carried his tail higher, and the arthritis medicine helped him move much more easily. He began smiling when he saw us and appeared to be finding his place in our pack.

By January 11th, Winston was ready for his surgery. Besides the neuter, he had eight teeth removed, and because his gums were worn down, he had a bone graft in his jaw. The vet brought him up-to-date on vaccines, and both of our veterinarians gave him a good prognosis.

Six months later, Winston is a happy dog. He follows me around the house and seems to love attention. I can honestly say that I have never received a Christmas present that I have enjoyed so much. I have had friends thank us for saving him from his dire situation. Actually, I feel he saved me from my doldrums and gave meaning to the Christmas season. He is truly the gift that keeps on giving.

 *Dan Curl*

Deer Beats Ball

Tucker is a very special dog who came into our lives 2½ years ago. We had two other dogs at the time, one who was particular about letting other canines into the house, but we decided to give Tucker a try. At first, we had no idea what to do with him, since he is paralyzed and incontinent, and we had never cared for a disabled dog. It took us about six months to figure everything out. My husband and I volunteer for Tennessee Valley Golden Retriever Rescue (TVGRR) located in Knoxville, Tennessee. A woman named Angel contacted our intake committee for assistance with a Golden Retriever she had rescued from a bad situation. She did not have the means to take care of this dog, as his back legs were paralyzed. He had been shot, and his owner had left him for dead. Could we help?

Our intake coordinator, Rachel, took videos of this paralyzed dog and sent them to the committee. With much trepidation, we said yes, we would take him and have him evaluated. For the next several days, Tucker stayed at our vet until we could figure out the best thing for him. We hoped the vet would be able to tell us if he was truly, permanently paralyzed, and if so, what special treatment he would need. We weren't even sure that he would be adoptable.

My husband and I discussed the issues extensively with our vet and ultimately decided to foster Tucker. We had built a ramp for one of our previous fosters, so Tucker would not have to navigate any stairs. Our vet knew someone who had an available doggie cart—their German Shepherd Dog had just passed away—so we were able to borrow the cart until we could see how this whole process was going to work. When TVGRR later decided to purchase a doggie cart for Tucker, we really felt like were on our way to saving this very special dog.

We struggled with where we were going to keep Tucker due to his incontinence. He still wanted attention, companionship, and the same loving treatment as the rest of our dogs. We bought a pen and special flooring, so Tucker had his own area in the house; we wanted him to be part of our family.

Tucker took to his wheels quickly. It did take him a couple of days to learn how to back up, but forward was no problem, which he reminded us of each time he saw a squirrel, deer, or tennis ball. We now know that Tucker will choose chasing a deer over a ball any day, but when the deer jumps the fence, he's back to the ball. (Of course, Tucker loses the ball in the deer chase, so we have to go back to the house for another ball.)

Occasionally Tucker does a "crash and burn," or rather, he tips his cart by going too fast for the terrain or taking too tight a turn. When this happens, he waits patiently for us to get him settled back in, and then off he goes again! That is, unless there is a deer involved. If the chase is on and Tucker falls over, he wiggles out of his cart and continues on with his front legs going as fast as they can and the rest of his body dragging behind. His cart has been lost in the woods on more than one occasion, so now we know to look for the cart and then for Tucker. Because this usually happens at dusk, we put red lights on the cart.

Many people are amazed to learn that Tucker loves to swim and that he *can* swim. In fact, we have four dogs (three Goldens and one black Lab), and Tucker is the best swimmer of all! Tucker loves to go down to the dock. He goes down the ramp into the water and wants us to throw the ball for him all day long. Tucker also loves boat rides. We have a favorite island with a sand bar where Tucker can chase the ball and then come back and "stand." When he's in the water, you would have no idea that Tucker is paralyzed.

We had been fostering Tucker for about 10 months—taking him to adoptathons and talking to people about him—when someone came to us and said that he knew of a person who might be interested in adopting Tucker. This brought tears to my eyes. Who else could love Tucker like we did? Who else could give Tucker the advantages he had at our house?

Although I did not say anything at the time, I knew that we could not let Tucker go to anyone else. Ours was the best home for him, as we have 10 fenced acres where he can chase deer, and we live on the lake where he can swim. Plus, six months after taking in Tucker, we adopted Kody, a Lab-mix adolescent who quickly became Tucker's playmate and best buddy. There's a special place in our home and hearts for Tucker, so we decided to adopt him ourselves.

Tucker has a great attitude; he is always happy, and he keeps us laughing. He loves kids, dogs, and even the cat. Tucker does not know he is disabled, and we certainly aren't going to tell him! He's a big hit wherever he goes, surprising people at events with his speed and agility. Tucker taught us that caring for dogs with disabilities is no big deal, and he continues to help us educate others about disabled dogs and the joy they can bring to a family.

 *Karin Jessen*

Special-Abled Anecdotes

Slinging Right Along: I saw a Facebook post about a two-year-old toy Poodle called Annabelle. In her photo, she was standing in a four-wheeled cart. She had been abandoned on the side of a busy road in California and lay there for days until she was spotted. She was completely flea infested and couldn't lift her head. A problem with the gray matter in her cerebellum, which controls balance, does not allow her to stand or sit upright without assistance. My husband and I decided to give her the chance she deserved. Once she was home with us, we could see that Annabelle wanted to follow our other two dogs and get exercise. My husband designed a sling that stabilizes her and allows her to go on our long walks with us. Having Annabelle as a pack member brings us joy every day, and everyone who meets her says she is an inspiration. We can't imagine life without her. *-Tami Stodghill*

Soldiering On: Ivy came from a backyard breeder who couldn't sell her because of her many physical problems, including incontinence, a malformed spine, and a disconnect between her brain and her hind legs. Hers is no heroic redemption story; she's got a waspish temper and doesn't like sharing us. She nips, emits ear-piercing barks, and has boundary issues. The money we've spent on ruined floors might have sent us on any number of European vacations. With that said, she's also the smartest, funniest, most loving dog we've ever known. She'll run, fall, and then drag herself by the front legs across a field in passionate pursuit of a ball. She gets up, or doesn't, but she soldiers on somehow. She doesn't just get by; she is on top of her game and full of boundless determination, and we would most certainly do this all over again. *-Tracy Huddleson*

Nothing Amiss

It's not obvious at first when you see the couple walking down the street with four Boston Terriers all keeping pace. When you see them doing therapy dog work at the hospital and the care home, you might not notice anything amiss. Even when that special Boston is practicing jumps, tunnels, and weave poles for agility or he's playing ball in the yard, you'd be hard-pressed to identify any issues, except that you may wonder, "Why isn't he running in a straight line to go and get the ball?"

Well, it's because he has no eyes.

♦♦♦

Tyke wasn't always this way. He was born with eyes and sight, and he grew up like any other dog on the block. He went to puppy class, where he did exceptionally well. He played ball, learned agility, swam in the lake, and walked on the treadmill when it was too cold in the winter to go out.

When Tyke was a year-and-a-half old, we started to notice that he had trouble finding his toys when we played fetch. To get some answers, we took him to the vet and then to the university for eye tests.

Cataracts.

We were devastated.

After we became accustomed to the idea, we decided that we wouldn't treat Tyke any differently than our other dog.

As our Bassett, Zeke, got older, and Tyke's eyesight grew dimmer, we decided to get another Boston. That way, Tyke would have a similar-sized "seeing-eye dog" when the time came to put Zeke down. Along came Willow.

Tyke and Willow did a lot of the same activities. One winter we did Rally-O (fun obedience done to directional signs), and Tyke passed with a higher score than Willow on the final test. Another winter we did On The Ball Therapy at the university. This entailed the dogs learning to balance on the wobble board and the balance ball and using the aqua treadmill to get core strength for agility. With patience, understanding, and unwavering trust, Tyke learned to do everything that was asked of him.

After Tyke's eyesight had failed to such a degree that we felt he should no longer compete in agility, we adopted Zeus.

You would think that between knowing this breed has eye problems and helping one of our own through the loss of his eyesight, we would have thought twice about getting a third Boston Terrier, but it never even crossed our minds.

When Tyke was seven, he was playing with one of his toys at Christmas, and he ended up puncturing an eye, which never healed and eventually ruptured. Because his cataracts were so far advanced, we decided to remove both eyes. Upon first seeing him with his eyelids sewn shut after the surgery, I broke out in tears, but I knew it had been the right decision.

Tyke still loves swimming in the lake or a pool as long as he has his life jacket on and his squeaky rubber duck to chase. He still does agility for fun and gets to practice every time his siblings work out. In the winter, when it's too cold to go outside, we do the treadmill, the balance ball, and the wobble board to keep him in shape.

We spend Monday nights doing St. John's Ambulance Therapy Dog work. Everyone is happy to see Tyke, and Tyke, in turn, is happy to see everyone. He offers himself for the hugs and scratches he knows he's going to get. Every time we visit, we get the question, "Is this the dog with no eyes?"

The university asked if we could give them a disc with pictures and video of Tyke doing all of his activities to help people see that blind dogs can still be active, loving family members. We did it gladly, and his dad went one step further. He created a Facebook page to help promote the fact that blind dogs can still do just about anything they set their minds to. To us, Tyke's blindness is not really a big deal, and in fact, we just adopted a little Boston girl who only has one eye.

I still get a big smile every time someone has to get down and look closely at Tyke's face to make sure I'm not kidding about his lack of eyes. It amazes them (and me, still) how well he manages without the sense that many of us take for granted.

 *Andrea Serack*

Cured by Canines

Tiny came into my life in a most unexpected way. I had recently lost my stepfather to diabetic complications. Shortly before that, I had been diagnosed with multiple sclerosis (MS), a debilitating disease that quickly stole my health. In short order, I found myself fighting for disability benefits as a very sick single mom of three young children.

One day I went to PetSmart during an adoption event, and while I was motoring around the store, a little Rat Terrier jumped into my lap with no fear of the chair whatsoever. Various other people wanted to visit with her, but she refused to leave my lap. I figured that the last thing I needed was another responsibility, but the rescue suggested I take her home as a foster to potentially adopt her. Well, it wasn't five minutes after I got home that I became a foster failure (I decided to keep her).

Approximately one month later, the rescue contacted me and asked me to consider fostering a pregnant Beagle, who was slated to be euthanized in a high-kill shelter. First I said no, but that lasted just seconds until I started to imagine what would happen to her. So Honey came to my home for a time.

The Rat Terrier I had adopted, Ping, had been a momma before, and she immediately took to being a doula to Honey. Honey was as sweet as her name, and she allowed Ping inside the cage where she was laboring. When the babies started arriving only a week or so after Honey's arrival, Ping was right there to help. The pups came so fast that Honey didn't have time to clean them quickly enough. I noticed that one pup was not breathing as I busily cleaned another. My eldest daughter, who was 14 at the time, grabbed her and immediately removed the remaining sack. She started chest compressions and even breathed into the pup's nose/mouth. As a result of my daughter's quick thinking, Spirit (as my daughter named her) survived and thrived.

Two of the pups were very small and didn't seem right. However, they nursed and Honey took care of them, so I figured they were probably fine (I wasn't a vet, so what did I know?). Unfortunately, at about two weeks of age, the pups developed Coccidiosis, a parasitic disease of the intestines, and two died.

The pair who didn't seem quite right managed to beat the Coccidiosis, but the vet told me they definitely had other problems. Dottie and Tiny, as we named them, both had hydrocephalus, or water on the brain. The vet advised me to immediately put them to sleep, though not without saying that since Dottie's case wasn't too severe, she might have a shot at living a relatively normal life. I asked if the pups were in pain and was told no, so I refused to put them to sleep. The vet said that Tiny would never be "pet quality," let alone trainable in any way. "So," I said, "then he will live whatever life he was meant to have right here with me. We'll be two disabled souls fighting for the best quality of life possible."

The vet was right about Dottie's chance at life, and I would never have forgiven myself if I had let him put her down. She stayed with me longer than the other pups just because I wanted to ensure that she was stable and healthy, but then she got adopted into a wonderful home. I heard that she adjusted well and that her new family loved and spoiled her. (The other pups also went to good homes, as did their momma, Honey, who went to live with a little girl who lost her dog in a divorce situation.)

As for Tiny, he stayed with me. At eight weeks old, he still weighed only one or two pounds and just couldn't seem to absorb any of the puppy food he ate. I began to experiment in my kitchen to try and help him. Boiled chicken. Rice. Scrambled eggs. Baby food meat. I cooked up various concoctions until we found something that would stick with him and help him grow. At eight months old, he was finally big and strong enough to be neutered, though for a Beagle, he was still very small.

When I first received the news about Tiny's hydrocephalus, I was sleeping on the couch in my living room because much of my house was not handicap accessible. Tiny slept cradled in my arms every night, and whenever he needed to potty, he would wake me. I would put him down on the floor, and he would head down the tile hallway and potty there before returning to me. In the morning when I got up, all I needed was a mop or a little tissue to clean up after him. Not trainable? Yeah, right. He did that part all on his own.

At a subsequent visit to our vet, I asked about Tiny's life expectancy. The vet said that since Tiny wasn't experiencing complications related to the hydrocephalus now that he was absorbing his food, there was no reason to expect anything less than a normal life expectancy. I nearly danced a jig right there.

Since Tiny was born, his presence has helped me to focus less on my disability and fears. Instead, my thoughts have been filled with joy about his successes and the baby steps he takes forward. (So what if it took two years to completely housetrain Tiny?) Between caring for Tiny, keeping a positive attitude, and leaving the stress of my job, I am now able to walk again like normal, and most people cannot tell that I have MS unless I discuss it with them. I would never have guessed that a little Rat Terrier jumping into my lap in

PetSmart would lead me to fostering a pregnant dog from a high-kill shelter. This chain of events ultimately helped guide me into remission and into living and loving life with a far greater appreciation than I had ever had before.

Today, Tiny still prefers to sleep in my arms at night. He weighs a healthy 25 pounds and is full of ornery. He has even learned a couple of obedience commands, and this October, he'll celebrate his seventh birthday!

 *Valerie Keener*

Invisible

Finn doesn't appear to have any disabilities at first glance, but that's only if you spot him before he runs away. His disability is the invisible kind—fear and anxiety—which, for a time, had him practically paralyzed.

This Spaniel-mix's wonderful foster mother, Emily, had found Finn curled in the back of a kennel. He was ignoring the outside world, awaiting euthanization in a high-kill shelter. At first, Emily had passed him by, leaving the shelter for her long trip home. When she later realized that the single overlooked pup would be one of the first to die, she called a nearby rescue and asked them to take Finn out of the shelter for her because she wasn't sure if she'd make it back in time. As soon as they got him out, Emily took him in as a foster.

According to his records, Finn had been collected from a hoarding situation with hundreds of other dogs in a single household. He had most likely been abused, as Finn is terrified of humans, especially males.

Emily spent a couple months working with Finn before I came across his picture on Petfinder.com. I'd been searching for a dog for a while by then, but I had yet to settle on one because I was nervous about whether I could handle a dog, let alone a special-needs dog, which is what my heart was calling for.

The moment I met Finn, my concerns melted away, and I knew he was the one for me. Sure, he ran from me at our first meeting, but perhaps that was the beauty of it. I felt the need to help him develop a better rapport with people and learn how to just be a dog.

It has now been eight months since I adopted Finn, and while he still has a long way to go, he's getting much braver. At first, he dodged interactions with my father and brother. He sat in his crate for the better part of the day and only came out briefly at night to eat and drink. He never barked, and I had to gently prod him to get him to do even the simplest of tasks.

It took a while to see any changes in Finn, but the efforts weren't in vain. Finn now comes and goes throughout the house as he pleases. He still needs to be on a leash outside every now and again because he gets scared easily, but he can usually roam freely. He's given me the pleasure of hearing his voice on a few occasions, and, for the most part, he acts like any other dog when he's around me. With strangers, it's a different story, but we're working on that.

Adopting and rehabilitating a special-needs animal is a long road. The decision to do so is not one that should be taken lightly, but the rewards of seeing a challenged animal live a happy life are worth the trial and effort.

 *Jessica Russell*

Bygone Boston

I n mid-February several years ago, I received two emails and a phone call regarding an "antique" Boston Terrier. All three stated that a man wanted to surrender a 19-year-old male. Nineteen! I called the older gentleman and was told that Mr. Dillon was, indeed, 19 years old, and he was also deaf and blind.

Mr. Dillon had originally belonged to a man in the auto sales business in Spokane, Washington. When Mr. Dillon's owner was drinking, the little brown dog often did without.

On a cold, snowy night in January two years earlier, Mr. Dillon was found under a motor home in the sales lot. He was curled up in his little red bed with a bag of dog food next to it. He was shaking so hard that his teeth were chattering. His owner had gone and left the little dog to fend for himself.

If Mr. Dillon hadn't been found that night, he would have died. His rescuer took him into his home and gave him a life that was quite the opposite of what he had been surviving. He had the run of the house, the best dog food, and regular visits to the vet.

People are funny, though, and this man now wanted to surrender Mr. Dillon to rescue simply because he "didn't want to watch him die." Of course, Boston Terrier Rescue of Western Washington didn't hesitate to take Mr. Dillon, though, honestly, we didn't know what to expect. A rack of bones? Totally gray? Deaf and blind! Whatever his condition, we vowed that Mr. Dillon would have the best remaining months of his life with us.

Boy, was I astonished when I saw Mr. Dillon! From out of the car came a plump, dark seal-brown, shiny-coated Boston Terrier with a few gray hairs on his face. His terrible breath and brown teeth betrayed his age, and his gait was awkward, though he moved surprisingly well. His eyes were almost totally clouded over, and he could hear, but just barely.

Our vet checked out Mr. Dillon and guessed that he was actually between 14 and 16 years old. We quickly learned that Mr. Dillon's favorite things to do were—imagine this— eat and sleep. He loved to have his rump scratched and danced a cha-cha when we scratched him. He went for short walks and played a mean game of tug-of-war now and then.

Mr. Dillon lived with us for two years and one month. He didn't quite make it to 19. We feel blessed to have shared our home with the sturdy little survivor. He worked his way into our hearts with his happy disposition and goofy smile. An antique? Maybe. He was an old gentleman with a heart of gold who left us with many fond memories.

 *Vicki Brunell*

O ne day I received a frantic call about a disabled Chihuahua who needed help. She was at a sanctuary located about two hours from me, where they were equipped to take in death-row dogs and find them homes but not to provide special care for injured animals. Could someone get this three-year-old, 10-pound dog to a veterinarian?

As the story goes, the Chihuahua's human mom had hit her with the car and paralyzed her back end. But the human mom didn't take the injured animal to a vet. She let the dog live in pain for more than two weeks before deciding to take her to the sanctuary.

Despite her predicament, this Chihuahua was just as sweet as a candied apple. She dragged herself around and smiled from ear to ear with her tongue curling at the tip. Though incontinent and helpless in many ways, she wouldn't let anything get her down, including her paralyzed back legs.

I took Lola in as a foster, and the little dog warmed my heart as well as that of my recently-adopted Great Dane, Arthur. Even though Arthur was 150 pounds and Lola was only 10 pounds, the pair chased each other and played tug of war. Lola was always determined; she would grab one end of the toy and let Arthur lift her into the air. He would swing her around like he was her amusement park ride; she loved it! Lola's poor little legs were getting chafed from being dragged around on carpet and cement, so I wrapped them in gauze. She was incontinent and therefore needed diapers, but she didn't like wearing them at all. Unfortunately, her continuous leakage of urine gave her burns on her skin, so I applied a special ointment to help her with that. Needless to say, she has endured a lot since her injury.

As I continued to care for Lola, I soon realized her bad habit: even though she had been hit, she couldn't stop herself from chasing cars. She went out of control when a car drove by. Suddenly, her tragic accident made more sense. To keep her safe on walks with Arthur and me, I put her in a baby carriage made for dogs with special needs. She was comfortable, zipped in, and able to see the world around her. She loved it!

Finding Lola a forever home was challenging. She needed an extra-special family that could care for her long-term needs, and they had to commit to her safety and keep her from chasing cars. I interviewed possible families and finally decided on a nice family with two young sons who were huge animal lovers. The entire family came over to meet Lola and loved her. They were approved for adoption about a week later, so on her way she went. Unfortunately, after a month, the family called and said that they felt that they weren't the best family for Lola, so they returned her to me.

Luckily, it didn't take long to find Lola another wonderful home with a woman named Carrie and her husband. The pair wanted to take Lola into their organization, Out to Pasture Farm & Rescue, which exclusively cares for special-needs animals. They adopt out some animals, but they are prepared for most to live with them for the duration.

Now, we had one hurdle left to jump, and it was a big one: How would we get Lola to Carrie's home in Connecticut from my home in Colorado?

One of my contacts found a flight attendant, Stephanie, who was willing to take Lola on the airplane with her if we could find someone to help her. She could provide a buddy pass for anyone who could accompany her, and my friend Lori, from Rocky Mountain Great Dane Rescue (RMGDRI), stepped up for the task.

We also had to find someone to meet the girls at the airport in Connecticut and then drive Lola to Out to Pasture Farm & Rescue, which was 2½ hours away. Our Connecticut friend, Maggie, and her niece, offered to take the two-hour trip to the airport to pick up Lola and take her to Carrie at Out to Pasture.

At the last minute, Lori couldn't go, so another RMGDRI board member, Lisa, offered. Everything else went off without a hitch, and hours later Carrie and her husband delightfully greeted Lola. That's when I knew that we had done the right thing, even though the journey took 10 people and many hours. Carrie later wrote me that her husband and Lola had bonded and that Lola had become "his girl." Apparently Lola now follows him everywhere.

While this story started out grim and hopeless for this little girl with a big smile, because of the big hearts she inspired to help her, she has moved on to greener pastures.

 *Robin Thompson*

Tag Team

When Frankie and Freddie joined our family, we immediately noted that Frankie was the muscle in the tag team. These two boys were so different—so opposite—yet so close, as brothers often are. Frankie was innocent and always getting "blamed" for things because of his size and his inability to look *not* guilty. Like Laurel and Hardy or Mutt and Jeff, this duo was always within each other's sight. One boy was always plotting and conniving, while the other was acting out the plan. Frankie was the protector and the follower, always seeking guidance from Fred.

When Fred left us, Frankie was lost, and a part of him never healed. This tag team had always been together. When their first family game them up, Golden Retriever Freedom Rescue took them in and then allowed us the opportunity to share our lives with them. These Golden oldies played rough and tough, supporting each other during each of their bouts with cancer and taking care of each other, just as they took care of us.

Frankie is truly a survivor. He won battles with cancer several times. Just two months after he adopted us, a cancerous tumor grew on his paw, eventually forcing the paw's removal. With the support of a brilliant surgeon/therapist from Sweden and of OrthoPets in Denver, Colorado, Frankie was fitted with a prosthetic limb. His therapist had a bit of an accent, so when she commanded him to put weight on the prosthetic, instead of saying, "Fix the foot," it came out more like, "Feeex da fooot." Frankie caught on quickly when *she* encouraged him to use his new foot in her charming accent, but when we said, "Fix the foot," he just gave us a confused look like *we* were speaking a foreign language! It was a while before we caught on and started mimicking the way his therapist would say it.

He took to the device quickly and never looked back. Running, swimming, hiking—no missing paw could stop Frankie on his mission to enjoy life to the fullest. Surely nothing ever stood in his way when it was time to make a beeline to his food bowl.

What a perfect patient Frank was. Food motivation sure helped, but he never put up a stink, always accepting the hand he was dealt and making the best of it. He looked at his situation not as a handicap but an opportunity to show people that *old dogs rule!*

This past year Frank battled mast cell cancer, which began as lesions on the skin. He endured with dignity two operations, numerous setbacks, and chemotherapy. Unfortunately, his recovery was not to be.

Our big man, our "leaner," our 5:30 a.m. alarm clock, has left us to join his brother. The emptiness and sadness are washed away not by our tears but by our vision that the boys are united once more and that "the posse" rides again!

Frankie, our class clown, our brave, innocent boy, listen to your bother and remember to "feeex da fooot"! Thanks for teaching us to seek out the opportunity in every challenge and to achieve happiness by maintaining a positive attitude and spirit.

Remember us, Frankie, we love you.

 *Carol Polacek*

Blind Love

Blind love. It's what we all hope for, is it not? We desire another to see us with total clarity without any of the noise that "seeing" actually creates. Blind love is a rare find, and I am blessed to have it. To say I found it would be a lie, as it fell into my life like a gift from heaven. I have found that it is the easiest thing to reciprocate because my blind love came in the form of my dog, Corra.

I adopted Corra after her first owner moved away and left her behind like unwanted garbage. Corra was almost destroyed by an archaic law that deemed all Pit Bulls "vicious," but a rescuer gave her a chance at a new life. She made it onto a list of adoptable dogs, which is how I found her. I had seen close to 20 dogs before seeing her, but I knew at first glance that she was the one. She loved other dogs; she didn't want toys or treats; and she just wanted to be with me.

Corra had luxating patellas (a genetic issue in which the kneecap doesn't fit properly into its groove) in both knees and required surgeries. She had pleurisy (an inflammation of the lining surrounding the lungs) for a week, but we luckily got in the first dose of antibiotics before she stopped eating. She recovered quickly, but something still seemed to be wrong. After her rabies booster shot, Corra licked feverishly at her front paws. Her strong front legs gave way, and she could barely stand. Her joints were the size of small oranges. We found out that she had lupus, an auto-immune disease that causes the body to attack itself.

We combated Corra's lupus with anti-inflammatory pills and pain killers, which she still needs daily. Imagine! Every day I stick my hand halfway down a Pit Bull's throat, only so that she may still walk! Like most Pit Bulls, she's a good patient. I just lightly tap on her teeth and say, "Open, baby doll," and she always does, despite trying her best to spit the pills forward once I'm done.

Having felt we beat the toughest of winters with both the pleurisy and the lameness, we all were looking forward to the warmth and hope that spring would bring. Then, one day in March I came home from work to be met at the door by only one dog (Tony, Corra's best doggie-friend). Knowing that something was amiss, I began searching for Corra. She always came when I called, but this time, I didn't hear the typical patter of her feet.

I found Corra on the couch with her front legs looking normal, and her rear legs stretched out as though she were waking them up and preparing them to carry her 50 pounds toward me. After I repeated my call, she moved slowly toward me and seemingly deliberately walked straight into a chair. It was then that I knew why she was struggling: she couldn't see me, or anything, anymore.

We fought Corra's blindness around the clock with multiple eye drops, but we couldn't control the pressure in her eyes. Despite our efforts, we came to the conclusion that there was nothing more we could do to save Corra's eyes from the disease; she required double enucleation, the complete removal of everything associated with her beautiful, big, brown eyes, which were regularly heralded as "stunning" by passersby.

After Corra's surgery, my husband, Tony, and I were joyous that we still had our Corra, though we were saddened when we thought about how Corra used to relish watching the world around her. Although she seemed at peace about the fact that she was no longer able to run around like the other dogs, we thought that she must feel left out when they ran away, and she couldn't keep up. She could only hear them; she was no longer able to enjoy watching them—or watching anything—ever again. Or so we thought.

Corra outsmarted us all. She quickly learned to act on verbal commands like easy (slow), EASY (full stop *now*), step down, and step up. She began to follow voices, clicks, and taps, which helps her to easily maneuver into the car, down the stairs, around the house, and on the trail. She finds the doggie door on her own and deftly moves the curtain in front of it aside with her nose. All by herself, she takes a few steps onto the deck and finds the ramp that takes her safely down to the yard to do her business.

Corra *loves* massages and even spreads out on the couch for them, flipping gently onto her back when she hears my husband's "torsional twist" command (he's an engineer). Her cute front paws dangle in the air, her back legs fully extend, and her loose lips pull back just enough to notify the entire world that indeed dogs *do* smile. She even lets out a couple pleasurable cooing moans.

If I touch the leashes, she comes as quickly as she can to stand with Tony on the stairs and wait for her leash to be snapped on. Perhaps she'll bump into one of the seven pillows that we've strewn across the floor to prevent her from having a collision with a sharp table corner or wall edge, but amazingly, she mostly uses her other senses to catch the flow of the air and adjust herself onto the correct path.

Although my husband and I have been laid off from work several times during the past four years, and Corra's medication costs $5 per day, we've always found the money there for her. For some, that's a cup a coffee; for us, it's another day of our precious Pit Bull's mobility. Corra pays us back in full every day with gentle, wet kisses. Her perky ears tilt to "see" us, and we feel like she's saying, "Don't worry! I can smell you, and I love you!"

Corra can tell if we are awake and ready to be "loved" by the changes in our breathing. At just the right time, she slowly moves her body between a dresser and the bed to remind us with gentle coos that she's here for us. That's when she gives us her gift—the gift to melt away our worries and to remind our souls about what's important. It's complete and total blind love with a side order of hope and trust. Corra's love makes me feel like I'm the one who has been rescued, and I'm grateful to spend another glorious day with my Pit Bull, who sees me with total, blind love.

From time to time, I miss Corra's eyes, and mine drift toward old pictures of her when she still possessed them. After a few difficult moments, my mind comforts me with the following thought: what I'm looking at is no longer Corra; the Corra I have now is even more precious and beautiful.

 *Susan Cavote*

Special-Abled Anecdotes

Not Going Down: One day I received a call from an Alaska Humane Society Adopt-a-Cat volunteer telling me about Zepplin, an incontinent cat who was unable to walk after being shot with a pellet gun. His family couldn't care for him, nor could Adopt-a-Cat. Would I be his foster? I had never cared for a cat in Zepplin's condition, but I took him in anyway because I wanted to help. Since then, I have learned a lot about caring for special-needs pets, and I've found Zepplin's strong will and tough but gentle spirit inspiring. Originally, I was only going to care for him until I could find him a forever home, but I came to love him so much that I decided the best forever home for him was with me. *-Corliss Kimmel*

Now in Need: Jake was a trained hearing dog for a deaf woman, who was a public speaker by trade. He had a lot of work to do, and he was good at being her ears. They grew older together, and when his person began to need more specialized care, Jake did, too, as his vision started to fail. Eventually, Jake went completely blind. When his guardian moved to a care facility, Jake moved in with me, as a foster dog for Blind Dog Rescue Alliance. He is a sweet, calm boy who deserves to receive the kind of care and love he used to provide to his human. We hope to find him a quiet retirement home soon.*-Kay Buffamonte*

No Big Deal

Liza, a Cavalier King Charles Spaniel, will melt your heart and greet you with a broad smile. She came to her foster family early last year when Cavalier Rescue USA asked if they would consider fostering a special-needs girl. Although they had never cared for a dog with special needs before, from day one, Liza taught them how to do it. Before coming into the rescue, Liza had several surgeries on her rear right leg, including one operation to have a metal plate and pins inserted for a broken leg, an operation for another break on the same leg, and an operation on her hip.

Her senior guardian could not keep up with her therapy program, and after her muscle tone atrophied significantly, a caring vet contacted Cavalier Rescue USA before the guardian could do the unthinkable.

Her foster family quickly found out that while Miss Liza is limited to doing a hip-hop-hobble on backyard outings, she is extremely motivated by food. If she knows there is food across the room, she will pull herself through an obstacle course to get to it! She loves lying around outside in the warm sun or cool shade, or lying around inside in their busy kitchen or office, just like any other dog. She also likes to swim, which is convenient since her foster family gives her water therapy in their pool or hot tub, or from time to time at a canine wellness program, where she displays her great swimming skill.

Water therapy removes the weight load on her injured limb and enables the gradual rebuilding of Liza's atrophied muscles. It reduces pain and accelerates recovery. Maintaining a therapy program is extremely important in Liza's case. She is taking medication for arthritis and occasional pain management, but in the water, no one can tell that Liza has any sort of disability.

This great little Cavalier passed a therapy dog certification, and with her foster family, she provided love and smiles to seniors, visiting them regularly in her doggie stroller.

Recently, Panda Paws Rescue (PPR) offered to take Liza in and provide her with whatever surgery and therapy she needs to have the highest quality of life. An organization called Wings of Rescue will fly her from California to PPR in Washington State, where she will swim at least three times a week. The organization is hopeful that they will be able to help her to walk on her own. Her mobility has been waning lately, so there is no time to waste!

 *Donna Beirne*

Angel's Angels

"Just bring them here..."

Those words began a journey that will probably last 10 to 14 years.

My poor sister, thinking she was doing the right thing, had a baby, moved to a new house, and adopted two rescue dogs, all in the space of three months. She did not cope well with the changes, and she felt terrible that the dogs weren't getting the love and attention they needed. After a month of watching their misery, my husband, in true animal-lover style, decided we should take the dogs and re-home them with suitable, loving guardians. We had recently lost three of ours to old age, so we had the space in our hearts and our home to have them for a "short time."

It was a good plan, except we quickly fell in love with the pair. And that's how Angel, a black-and-white German Short-haired Pointer, and Charlie, a Border Collie/Labrador-mix, came to live with us. Evidently, we were the suitable, loving guardians!

To say Charlie and Angel were broken is an understatement. They cowered constantly. Obviously, before the dogs had arrived at my sister's house, they had been abused by feet, hands, brooms, and spatulas, as they were terrified of them all. Neither dog would dare enter our house; we had to carry them inside at night, as we are firm "dogs inside at night" people (both for their safety from criminals and because it has been proven that indoor dogs are far greater deterrents against criminals). Within a week, Charlie had realized that this was heaven on earth. She quickly learned to accept love as freely as she gave it. We renamed her "Jelly" because she just wobbled with joy. She began smiling and talking and has never stopped.

Angel was a different story. Her abuse at her first home had apparently been more prolonged and severe. She is a strange dog; she does not learn under pressure, and because of that, she probably ended up suffering a lot of beatings during her "training." She learns at her own speed, which is quite slow. The poor girl is not the brightest spark in the fire! After eventually realizing she was allowed inside, crossing every threshold in the house became a major mission; she would not move from room to room. She finally understood that the sofa in the TV room was a safe zone, so she would scamper through the door and hop straight onto the sofa, freezing there with fear-filled, bloodshot eyes.

Having Angel spayed was a major breakthrough. She came home still pretty out of sorts from the anesthesia and subsequently wandered upstairs and onto our bed. From that day forward, our bed has been her safe place. It's there that Jelly and Angel get love, cuddles, kisses, and playtime. It took Angel a year before she finally rolled over and showed us her tummy for scratches, but now she lives on her back with her velvet spotted tummy open for love.

To help this pair over their fears, we read books and followed numerous tips on desensitizing animals, all to no avail. We eventually gave up and just loved them with all our hearts. That turned out to work better than any of the recommended therapies! Angel is still skittish about loud noises, but she is also incredibly loving and affectionate. She is one of those dogs you can lie on and drape your legs over. Any contact with your body is regarded as love. I "attack" her by head-butting her, biting her, growling at her, and pinning her down. She responds by smacking me with her paws and then rolling over and huffing at me.

Jelly is, well, I cannot put her into words. She is so intuitive it's bizarre. She can be instructed with a nod or shake of the head and a look in the eyes. That must be the Border Collie in her. Her favorite position is what we have named "air-ass," when she sticks her butt in the air and her head on the ground, waiting for a scratch. Three years later, we still laugh when she does it. She is very protective of me as her mommy. She adores her daddy, too, and while we watch TV, she lies on his lap, on her back while he scratches her tummy, or she cuddles up on his shoulder (keep in mind that we are talking about a 50-pound dog).

We never planned to take these two on. We had wanted to sell our house and move into a complex with our two small dogs (also rescues), but heaven had other plans. Angel and Jelly have taught us so much about love, patience, tolerance, and faithfulness. They fill our lives with deep joy and satisfaction. This is the reward of rescue dogs.

 *Brigitte Bell*

Decimal Place From Death

Sidecar (previously known as Chewie) is a sweet, brave, funny, fearless, 4.7-pound Yorkie/Maltese-mix. He came into my life just three short months ago. I was not looking for another dog. I had two rescues already, but something made me check the Florida Yorkie Rescue (FYR) website. My Barney had come from FYR, and from time to time, I would find myself perusing their website. That day they had posted a YouTube video about a dog name Chewie; it made me cry for an entire weekend.

Chewie's original owner decided one day that she didn't want him anymore. She literally threw him out in hopes that he would run away. He didn't. He was found shivering and scared at her doorstep the next morning. Imagine his terror and confusion! He must have been wondering, "Why doesn't she want me? What is going to happen to me? What did I do wrong?"

One of the woman's co-workers offered to take Chewie but noticed that he had a badly hurt front leg. Chewie wouldn't walk on it and whimpered when it was touched. The woman said simply, "He's okay. I just stepped on him."

Chewie was clearly better off without her, but now he needed immediate medical care. The woman's co-worker took Chewie to an SPCA veterinarian, who found that Chewie's ankle was shattered. He didn't have enough money to pay for surgery, so the vet put Chewie's leg in a splint and prescribed 50 mg of Tramadol (a mild narcotic) for pain. Chewie refused to take the medicine, which must have been a blessing from a guardian angel, because the proper dose was .5 mg, not 50 mg. That amount would have killed him!

Realizing he was in over his head, the man surrendered Chewie to FYR, whose volunteers took him to an orthopedic veterinarian immediately. Sadly, the only thing that could be done by now was to remove Chewie's left front leg and shoulder socket.

After his surgery, we adopted Chewie and renamed him Sidecar. He has since recovered completely, and he gets around quite well. He plays with our other fur babies, Higgins and Barney, and when he gets to the top of the waitlist for a doggie wheelcart, he'll be able to take longer walks with us.

Next month Sidecar will start training to become a therapy dog. This sweet dog's job will be to bring comfort and inspiration to those who need it most. This forgiving soul adores attention and is such a lap dog that we considered renaming him "Velcro," so we're confident that he will excel at his therapy tasks. What better way to make sense of his injury than to use it for something positive for him and for others?

 *Paula Gossett*

Remembering House and Home

Welcoming a blind dog into our home has been one of the most awesome things I have done. I had never really considered it before because my husband and I assumed that it might be a constant struggle. Even so, we adopted blind Taffy after meeting her through a friend who was fostering her for a rescue organization.

Immediately, Taffy fascinated us with her uncanny ability to manage and thrive, despite having no sight. Memorizing her environment is part of her survival instinct, and, of course, she relies heavily on smell and touch; in the beginning, sound also gave her direction, but her hearing faculties have recently declined. She uses landmarks on the ground to identify where she is, so we help her by creating as many as possible, such as mats at doorways and rug runners around the house. She walks in a straight line when we are outside by following the edges of sidewalks, and she knows the difference between the asphalt roadway and the cement edging just before the curb, which indicates to her when to step up.

From the beginning, I talked to Taffy much as you would a toddler. We consistently repeated the same words for various hazards and saw that Taffy was listening, remembering, and using our warnings to navigate. Simple commands like left, right, up, and down expanded into quick right, quick left, big up, big down, door's open, back up, nose up, bumpy, slippery, and careful among many others. As she committed these commands to memory, I was able to take Taffy for walks on a forest path with its varied terrain, where she could even climb over fallen logs. Our initial concern was that Taffy would walk into something sharp and get poked in the eye, which could lead to infection. Constantly watching her was a challenge, but deep down we were holding on to hope that we would be able to give her back her sight. Eventually, we had to have her eyes removed because they couldn't be repaired nor her vision restored, and they were causing her pain. We accepted that blind was how Taffy would always be, and once her eyes were removed and the pain was relieved, we found that she had more energy, and her quality of life increased dramatically. Our life became simpler, too, as we no longer had to concern ourselves as much with sharp objects.

In our own home, Taffy can wander. She goes up and down stairs, finds her water, food, and bed, and initially even got on and off the couch on her own. She loves to be outside, so we put in a dog door that we hoped she could use. Oh, how we cheered when she used it on her own for the first time! It gave her the freedom to choose where she wanted to be. Taffy doesn't play fetch, but other than that, life for her and for us was pretty much the same as it would be with a sighted dog. We don't rearrange furniture often, but we can do so if necessary. It just takes time for Taffy to learn the change.

At other people's homes, we either have to guide Taffy around, or she'll just find a safe place and stay there, not exploring as most dogs might do. When people notice this, they sometimes question her quality of life, but once they see her in her own environment, they understand what a treasure she is and how much she is able to do.

Taffy was with us for five years when we decided to relocate. We worried about how Taffy would feel about having to learn a completely new home and wondered if it was even the right thing to do. Taffy was now older and her hearing was failing. Additionally, we were seeing signs of confusion at times, and although we still talked to her constantly, we weren't always sure if she heard or understood us.

Nevertheless, we moved. The real estate agent had great fun with our list of dog needs, and we ultimately chose a home and yard that we thought would be suitable for Taffy. In her new environment, this wonderful little girl surprised us yet again with her adaptability, and we think she is just as excited as we are by the change. We brought items she used as guides and set up parts of the house to be as familiar as we could. We even widened the back stairs to be the same as what she was used to. It only took about a month for Taffy to really become confident and for us to be able to relax and just let her go.

Nowadays, we are back to our normal routine along with some new adventures, and Taffy is thrilled. In the old house, she stopped jumping up on the couch, perhaps due to her old age, but now she begs us to put her back up there. She stands with her nose pressed to the couch until we notice, and if we don't get to her fast enough, she gives us a little snort to tell us to pay attention. If we wander away, a small bark alerts us when she wants to get down. She can always tell when we are too far away to see her.

The new house is a bungalow, so it is easier for Taffy to get around. She explores more than she did in the old house and even chooses different rooms for naps. This summer we will try to duplicate her favorite flower bed from the old home, so she can again have her favorite place to nap in the yard. She seems to be searching for it.

Because we chose not to overlook a dog with vision limitations, even though we had our reservations, our lives have been enriched in countless ways. Taffy has adapted to whatever changes have come her way, and our experience with her has been exactly the opposite of burdensome. In fact, it has been one of the most rewarding experiences we have ever had. Her successes, even small ones, have filled us with love. Every day she makes us smile, laugh out loud, and sometimes even cry with joy. Whichever way you "look" at it, our house just wouldn't be a home without her.

 *Karen Welk*

Safe at Last

This story begins more than a decade ago. We were looking for a playmate for our two-year-old Boston Terrier, Mugsy. I began searching the Internet and found a page called Boston Terrier Puppy Mill Rescue. It featured adoptable Boston Terriers that had been rescued from a Midwest puppy mill, where they had been used as breeding machines and then discarded for no longer being "useful."

I sent in an application for Trixie, and after we were approved, a network of truckers transported her from Kansas to us in Waterbury, Connecticut.

Neglected and abused doesn't begin to describe the life Trixie must have endured. She was terrified and withdrawn. Her paperwork said that she had been born four years earlier, but she looked about twice her stated age. For one thing, she walked as if she were a senior, arthritic dog because she had spent her entire life in a cramped, chicken-wire cage

The first day, when we gave Trixie a bath, we scooped out as much dirt and bacteria from her ears as we could without hurting her. The vet gave us an antibiotic for her ear infection and informed us that 11 rotten teeth had to be removed. When she first came to live with us, Trixie ate her own stool, but when she realized that we would provide her with abundant food and water, she stopped. She also had a habit of frequently licking her splayed paws. We adopted Trixie in June, but it took several months for her to get used to us. She was terrified of loud bangs and flyswatters. Every step she took in those first few months was tentative and unsure. This new life of comfort and kindness was foreign to her. To help her adapt, we placed her dog bed in a corner of the living room so that no one could sneak up on her, and we tried to help her move forward at her own pace.

As pathetic and sad-looking as she was when we got her, Trixie did eventually come to realize that she was safe. I soon had a dog attached to my hip all day and night. She became Mugsy's boss while they enjoyed each other's company.

Our first trip to the local park is fresh in my memory, probably because it was the first time Trixie walked freely and was able to explore. She never got used to walking with a leash attached to a collar around her neck but became comfortable enough with a harness. Trixie loved car rides and going to the park. She was a wonderful travel companion when we took the dogs to Vermont and New Hampshire on hiking vacations. While she never fully recovered from the deep psychological and emotional scars of the puppy mill experience, she blossomed with our family and gave us more love and happiness than she could ever realize. Every roll in the grass, every tail wag and butt shake...we celebrated the simple things along with her.

When I had my first child in 2005, Trixie was a good mama. She got up for middle-of-the-night feedings and was always curious as to what the baby was doing.

Sadly, we had to say goodbye to our Trixie Belle the following year due to illness. Our time together was far too short, her freedom and joy too brief, but I rest easy knowing that she felt love and kindness in the years she was with us.

 *Claudia Miller*

She's No Sailor

On a cold winter's morning, young Kay-Lynn was found crying in the snow on our street in Brooklyn. She was so tiny and alone that my partner immediately scooped her up and brought her inside his apartment to warm up. She began purring immediately and allowed him to inspect her. My partner noticed fleas and the possibility of worms, but most alarmingly, he saw that she fell down when she tried to walk. Assuming that she was young and still getting her "sea legs," my partner took her to the vet for a regular wellness check-up.

The vet told him that her issue was not a case of growing pains. In fact, Kay was born with cerebral hypoplasia, or an underdeveloped cerebellum, which was likely genetic or perhaps brought on by her mother ingesting a poisonous substance. Typical of the natural order of things, when Kay's feline family had moved on, they left her behind because she failed to keep up due to her decreased motor skills.

The vet assured us that Kay would be fine and would grow up to be as healthy as one could expect if we treated her as we would treat any other cat, but she would always stumble and drunk-walk, and her ability to get on and off things would be significantly limited. Kay's spaying was a bit nerve-racking since she required an extremely skilled veterinarian to monitor the amount of anesthesia she was given, but luckily she got through it with flying colors.

Aside from a couple of broken teeth due to falls in her early years, Kay has proven to be healthier than even her normally-developed adopted brother. She has her own set of stairs to get on and off the bed, and we bring her up on the couch with us when she wants to be part of the group. She is as happy as any pet I've ever met, or maybe even happier because she seems truly grateful. She is incredibly low-maintenance compared with her hyperactive brother. I call her an angel, and I thank the universe every day for bringing her to us.

 *Peggy Kaplin*

Farm Called Forever

My name is Boston Riley. I was found a week after the Boston Marathon bombings, so I got the name "Boston" in memory of all who lost limbs during that tragic event. As for the "Riley" part, the name means valiant and courageous, so why wouldn't you name me that?

I don't really remember how I ended up this way; all I know is it hasn't been an easy hop. At six weeks old, I was a frightened puppy hopping around on a busy highway near Tokai, in the western cape of South Africa. The vets who examined me believe that my left paw was either chopped or bitten off (you wouldn't want to remember that either!). Bad things are known to happen in the area where I was found, so maybe I was lucky to get out of there with just a missing paw.

An angel named Helene stopped for me; I do remember that. She took pity on me as I flopped and flailed, and she scooped me up in her gentle hands and held my pounding heart close to her own. She whispered love into my ear and promised to find me a home that would keep me and love me forever. She sent out the call far and wide, and people everywhere read my story.

As the hunt for my forever family began, my angel of hope (as I call Helene) and her mother, the very loving Linda, took me in. Linda wore me around like a scarf, and they both provided me with a sense of protection, safety, and specialness. They even had a four-legged friend for me to play with, a Pit Bull pup named Joob. It was the first time I felt really safe and loved; it was wonderful.

Far away on the east coast of Natal (an eastern province of South Africa) the call about me was heard and heeded. The McNeils read about my plight and placed an urgent request to adopt me. They were approved, and shortly thereafter, I was on my way to them on an airplane! What's even cooler, my new home is on a farm actually called "Forever."

Now, here's my secret that I'll share only with you: since birth, I have possessed a super power called hope! Hope does not need four paws to start over. Hope rebuilds no matter what. Hope grabs you by your heart, with a spirited force much larger than any tragedy, and it carries you into your future. It drops you into a brand new life, where you get to learn new skills, new habits, and new thoughts. My hope is front and center, despite how hopeless my situation may have first appeared, and it has allowed my life to rebuild into something I never could have imagined.

You can use this super power, too. First you have to believe, believe that life has more good in it than bad. What my family and I have learned is that even when bombs explode or people do unspeakable things to injure and hurt animals or people, if we stand together and believe in hope, our lives become beautiful again. Just like mine has, and I am on a mission to pay it forward—forever!

 *Boston Riley (Translated by Sharyn McNeil)*

About Happy Tails Books™

Schnauzer   Chihuahua   Golden Retriever   PUG
DACHSHUND   German Shepherd   Collie   Boxer
Labrador Retriever   Husky   Beagle   ALL AMERICAN
Border Collie   Pit Bull Terrier   Shih Tzu   Miniature Pinscher
Chow Chow   Australian Shepherd   Rottweiler   Greyhound
Boston Terrier   Jack Russell   Poodle   Cocker Spaniel
GREAT DANE   Doberman Pinscher   Yorkie   SHEEPDOG
ST. BERNARD   Pointer   Blue Heeler

Happy Tails Books™ was created to support animal rescue efforts by showcasing the love and joy adopted dogs have to offer. With the help of animal rescue groups, stories are submitted by people who have adopted dogs, and then Happy Tails Books™ compiles them into breed-specific books. These books serve not only to entertain but also to educate readers about dog adoption and the characteristics of each specific type of dog. Happy Tails Books™ donates a significant portion of proceeds back to the rescue groups that help gather stories for the books.

Happy Tails Books™

To submit a story or learn about other books Happy Tails Books™ publishes, please visit our website at http://happytailsbooks.com.